I0415087

# small town,
# BIG PROBLEM

*Solutions for Homelessness*

By

Phil Johncock

ISBN: 9781087099217

# Table of Contents

# Testimonials

Phil Johncock is a master at telling his story of a small town addressing a big challenge to serve the homeless. It gives a clear path for other small towns who want to serve homeless individuals while also building up and serving the community. This is a must-read for communities in crisis seeking solutions.

~Chad McComas, Executive Director, Rogue Retreat

Brilliant! No matter the population size, every American city is gravely afflicted by an epidemic called HOMELESSNESS. Despite efforts of government, nonprofit, for-profit, faith-based and other agencies -- each struggling to discover, design, and facilitate solutions -- the sociological affliction continues to expand. *Small town, BIG PROBLEM* offers a thought-provoking insight into the lives of displaced persons, as well as an analysis of why solution-oriented programs are failing. It is a comprehensive guide for community rehabilitation.

~Joseph Galata, Sierra Association of Foster Families

Phil Johncock is a Homeless ROCKSTAR!

~Kelly Madding, City Administrator, City of Ashland

This is really good work. *small town BIG PROBLEM* tells an important story of incremental progress - and the need for more. What I love about it is that it is a template for moving the ball forward - and it speaks so well to the teamwork required to do so. We've made progress over the years. We've made the most progress when everyone pulled together ... and that will be even more true as we move forward into the future.

~Dennis Slattery, Councillor, Ashland City Council

Phil Johncock's *small town BIG PROBLEM* provides a practical and comprehensive guide communities can use to create solutions of their own. Phil shows that creating successful programs that work toward ending homelessness can and must be done.

~Kacky Hoffman, Retired School Psychologist, Ashland, OR

Wow! You're on to a very strong solution with *small town BIG PROBLEM*. It succeeds in breaking the old paradigm that separates our communities into "Us vs Them." Thank you for writing this primer for social justice at the most basic human level, our need for shelter. I'm humbled to gain an early insight into what can become America's best opportunity to solve our fastest growing social crisis. Thank you, Phil, for galvanizing an outline for success which sheds light on the answers to homelessness in our communities. Well done!

~Troy Brown, Business Owner, Ashland, Oregon

# Dedication

This book is dedicated to our Ashland unhoused neighbors, many who participated in Ashland's Winter Shelter from November 11, 2018 through April 13, 2019:

- 129 were screened.
- 102 stayed at least one night or self-exited before entering.
- Due to fire code requirements, we could accommodate up to 34 "guests" per night.

One highlight for me was receiving a bouquet of 34 flowers (one flower representing one guest) at the end of the 2018-19 winter shelter season:

Even more special is that these beautiful, multi-colored flowers were hand-made by Wally, an artist who happened to be a shelter guest. Check out Wally's art at **facebook.com/wallace.foreverflowers**.

# Foreword

It has been my observation and my experience that in far too many places – whether big cities or small towns – the challenge of helping the homeless is not being met. Every day, ever more people are finding themselves without shelter, without food, without even a place to attend to their biological needs with dignity.

Too often, the Unhoused are treated as if they were criminals, as if they've done something wrong, as if they're unworthy of compassionate assistance—or of even being *noticed*. People walk right past them, eyes averted, hearts closed, pace slightly quickened, hoping to slip by without having to make any kind of eye-to-eye connection.

I'm not making this up. I've experienced it. Firsthand. I was homeless for a year, and without getting into the details of my personal story, I can tell you that there wasn't much assistance to be found. That was 25 years ago in Ashland, Oregon, where it was a major luxury to have the ability to take a shower or launder clothes—to say nothing of actually spending a night in a warm bed.

So much of that can change now, thanks to what is a virtual blueprint offered to us by Phil Johncock, who reports here on the many things that have been done in Ashland—solutions that are transferable to any town, large or small.

I am encouraged, uplifted, and inspired by what I have found on these pages: a treasure chest of tools, approaches, ideas, and practical, workable solutions surrounding the challenge of providing a compassionate response to the homeless in our communities.

Thank you, Phil, for this valuable contribution.

Neale Donald Walsch
Best-Selling Author of *Conversations with God*

# Introduction

*"We have come dangerously close to accepting the homeless situation as a problem that we just can't solve."*
~Linda Lingle, 6th Governor of Hawaii

## Problem

Here's the problem...

"Homelessness" may actually be the single greatest problem with which communities -- big urban and small rural ones -- across the United States of America are unable to solve! Consider these comments from people some of whom you may actually recognize:

- "This (homelessness) is the No. 1 issue in every city in California." ~Mayor Eric Garcetti of Los Angeles
- "Being homeless is like living in a post-apocalyptic world. You're on the outskirts of society." ~Frank Dillane, Actor
- "The biggest misconception about the homeless is that they got themselves in the mess - let them get themselves out. Many people think they are simply lazy. I urge those to make a friend at a local mission and find out how wrong these assumptions are." ~Ron Hall, Writer
- "We live in a world where there is so much wealth. There shouldn't be a homeless person. That's crazy." ~Raheem DeVaughn, Singer
- "Government alone cannot solve the problems we deal with in our correctional facilities, treatment centers, homeless shelters and crisis centers - we need our faith-based and community partners." ~Dirk Kempthorne, US Senator
- "Support for shelters and transitional living and housing programs is necessary if we are going to change the landscape for homeless boys and girls in America." ~Jewel Kilcher, Singer-Songwriter

It may come as a surprise to discover that even famous people have been homeless or close to it:

- "Was I always going to be here? No, I was not. I was going to be homeless at one time, a taxi driver, truck driver, or any kind of job that would get me a crust of bread. You never know what's going to happen." ~Morgan Freeman, Actor

- "I've been writing lullabies since the beginning. I kind of did it for myself to help myself fall asleep when I really worried, like when I was homeless and I'd fall asleep in my car." ~Jewel Kilcher, Singer-Songwriter
- "I've been homeless. I've worked at 7-Eleven." ~Dennis Rodman, Basketball Player
- "Before I was making music, I was homeless. I didn't have all the girls or any friends..." ~PnB Rock, Singer
- "I didn't mean to be a songwriter; I just was writing for fun, you have all day to do it. I was homeless so that's all I had to do." ~Jewel Kilcher, Singer-Songwriter
- "I was going to some fabulous party, and my taxi got stuck in traffic, and I looked out the window, and I saw a homeless woman rooting through the garbage, and I realized it was my mother. And I was so mortified that I ducked down, and I hid." ~Jeannette Walls, Author & Journalist

As you will discover in My Story (the next section), according to local residents of Ashland, Oregon, "homelessness" was indeed the single, greatest problem that was not being solved in our small town with a population of a little over 21,000.

Fortunately, Ashland, like many communities, had the willingness and even a pool of aging volunteers. What was missing though were three (3) steps as well as three (3) primary shifts of focus -- important "mindset" shifts -- that needed to happen, all that you will discover in this book.

If "homelessness" is indeed the greatest problem in your town or community, efforts to solve this BIG PROBLEM will be less-than-optimal without these three (3) steps and three (3) mindset shifts.

Let's change that! Let's give you the three (3) steps and three (3) mindsets you need to be successful!

Next up is My Story...

Enjoy!

Phil Johncock
Consultant
Ashland, Oregon

# My Story

*"In the middle of difficulty lies opportunity."* ~Albert Einstein

## It Was January 31, 2016...

But not a good day to be on the road. Unfortunately, I was. Mine was one of the few vehicles passing cars that had slidden into ditches, a result no doubt of a major snowstorm travelling through the western United States.

Thankfully, I had some help: four-wheel drive and a U-Haul trailer weighed down with my most important personal belongings inside. Driving slow helped, too.

The destination was my new home of Ashland, Oregon.

I was on a "Pilgrimage of Service" to see how I could be of service to Dr. Jean Houston, an Ashland resident, who just happened to be one of the principal pioneers of the human potential movement.

Jean was 78 at the time and Chancellor of Meridian University. I helped her create a nonprofit 11 years ago -- International Institute for Social Artistry -- but had to resign from the board when I threw out a disc in my lower back and couldn't travel to meetings.

As a result of my pilgrimage and working as a consultant with the Jean Houston Foundation:

- We offered an 8-day Social Artistry Leadership Institute on July 30 - August 7, 2016, at Southern Oregon University. Jean and Peggy Rubin were the primary teachers.
- We raised over $162,000 for Jean's foundation.
- More than 400 people attended some part of the Institute. 100 attended all 8 days from as far away as Nepal.
- I repurposed audio recordings of the 8-day Institute to create a "Game Changer" self-study course for 36 Continuing Education (CE) credits for licensed health professionals.

As I worked on Foundation business, I also began meeting many local residents of Ashland.

I decided to ask them the BIG QUESTION!

# The BIG QUESTION

To begin to "put down roots" and live long-term in this beautiful, Ashland community, I committed to wrapping my arms around the largest problem with which most people were struggling. "I will take this opportunity," I told myself, "to see what kind of difference I can make in my new community." This book is about the magic that happened next.

I began asking the same question of everyone I met:

**"What's the single biggest problem that Ashland cannot solve?"**

The answer came back the same… **"Homelessness!"**

It was the #1 answer everyone gave. There wasn't even a close #2!

I began meeting regularly with two amazing Ashland residents: Kathleen Hering, a local social activist, as well as Oshana Catranides, a local grant writer. We were on a mission to find what I called "Legal, Safe Places for People to Sleep and Shit" (LSPPSS). We (or really I) affectionately called our group "LSPPSS" because of the funny way it sounded when I tried to say it. It makes me chuckle even today when I say it.

Kathleen had been in Ashland a year or two longer than I. She had a few contacts working on homeless issues to whom she introduced me. One was Heidi Parker, who managed volunteers for Ashland's Winter Shelter. The shelter was run completely by volunteers four-nights-a-week during the coldest months of the year from mid-November through mid-April.

I went to the Orientation for volunteers in November 2016 and volunteered as an overnight host-in-training and then as a co-host for a half-dozen or so nights during the 2016-17 season.

In July 2017, Kathleen and I began meeting more regularly with Heidi who expressed an interest in retiring from her job as Volunteer Coordinator for the winter shelter, now entering its 10th year. In one of our first meetings, I mind-mapped how the winter shelter worked with coordination of services community-wide:

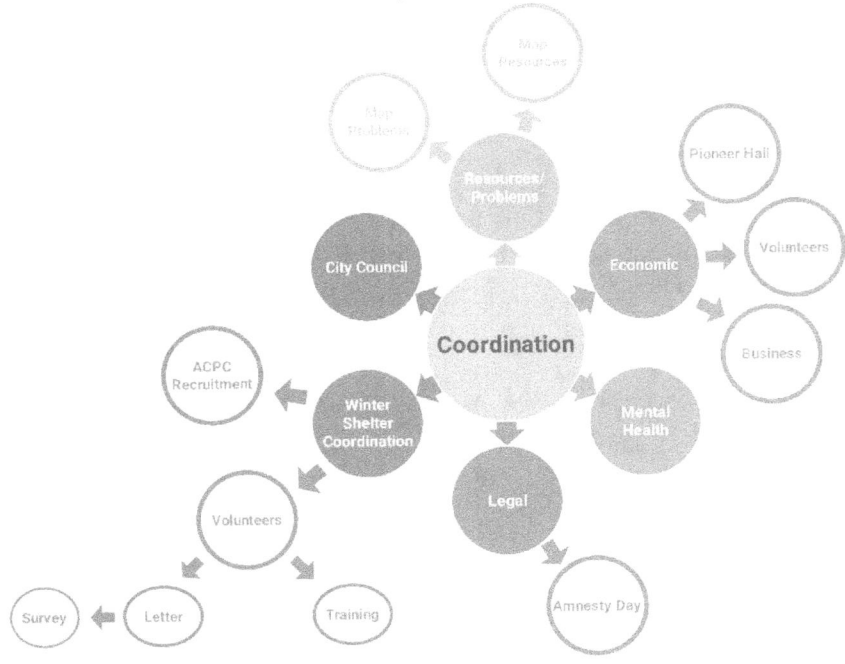

During the upcoming 2017-18 winter shelter season, Kathleen and I looked for ways to support Heidi such as helping her with the Orientation for new volunteers, making suggestions to expand the online signup form for volunteers, and setting up training with Peter Buckley on the topic of Adverse Childhood Experience (ACE) and its impact on homelessness and drug addiction.

# Story: Manifesting Funding for Heidi's Replacement

One of the jobs I agreed to take on was to help find funding to hire a person to replace Heidi.

The first thing we did was to help document what it was that Heidi actually did as a Volunteer Coordinator. I began meeting regularly with Heidi to talk about what she did. As a result, she shared documents, experiences, advice, tips, etc. We came up with a job description for her replacement. In January 2018, she transferred to me her "contact list" of volunteers (names, emails, phone numbers, notes).

"Now, watch," I thought to myself. "Funding will come!"

Sure enough, it did, too! In fact, it was the very next day after she passed on her contact list to me. She got a phone call from a funder who said, "We've got $25,000 in funding for a 'housing first model' shelter. Your winter shelter is one of the only eligible ones in Jackson County. Could you use the funding?"

Hmmm....

# 2017-18 Ashland Winter Shelter Season

We were still in the middle of the 10th season of winter shelter in Ashland. Money and a replacement would not be available until... well, we didn't actually know when. We did expect that money would probably not be available for a while. There was still a shelter to run with Heidi at the helm.

The 2017-18 Ashland Winter Shelter ran from November 12, 2017, to April 5, 2018. There were many significant accomplishments, too:

- Volunteers donated 3,915.5 hours (value = $94,520.17) for 123 nights of "no frills" shelter for 35-50+ unhoused guests/night, depending on each site's occupancy limit. Unfortunately, many guests had to be turned away due to reaching full capacity.
- Volunteers filled 270 co-host and trainee jobs (some staying all night, often at least 12 hours) and 317 listener, meal preparer/server, clean up crew jobs (1-1.5 hours).
- We started the season with four nights of shelter per week and ended with six nights of shelter. A huge THANK YOU to First Presbyterian Church of Ashland and Trinity Episcopal Church for allowing us to use their facilities for a night each of shelter as well as Ashland Mayor John Stromberg, Ashland City Councilors, City staff persons and Parks Department for the use of Pioneer Hall as the shelter site for four nights and emergency (Saturday) nights!
- A special thank you to the winter shelter Site Coordinators for stepping up to the massive undertaking of coordinating set up, food delivery and servers, trainees, guest volunteers, clean up, etc. -- again-and-again -- 6 nights per week (7 nights per week on 3 occasions) for 21 weeks: Bob Altaras, Karen Amarotico, Mary Bonney, Mark Goodman-Morris, Sharon Harris, Jason Houk, Vanessa Houk, Joan Kalvelage, Peter McBennett, Bob Morse, Alexandra Reid, John Wieczorek.
- We were especially grateful for the support of our community partners: Unitarian Universalists (UU's), United Congregational Church of Christ (UCC), South Mountain Friends Meeting (Quakers), First Presbyterian Church, Temple Emek Shalom, Trinity Episcopal, Southern Oregon Jobs With Justice and The City of Ashland.

One highlight for me was recognizing Heidi's six years of service managing volunteers at the Volunteer Appreciation Party on April 17, 2018, (she is sitting, holding the plaque and flowers):

# Hiring Heidi's Replacement

It took seven months for the job announcement for the Volunteer Coordinator position (Heidi's replacement) to finally be posted. Much had happened in the Ashland community between January 2018 (when Heidi first got the call of a $25,000 gift) and August 2018. We had lost Pioneer Hall as a winter shelter venue but we created the Group of 5 and a One Site committee of social activists on a mission to find a single location for winter shelter and create a new model. More about that shortly.

I was not initially interested in applying for the replacement position either. Nonetheless, Heidi kept encouraging me to apply. I had put in hundreds, perhaps over a thousand, of hours including being the chairperson for the One Site committee. "You're putting in the time anyway," she said. "You basically wrote the job description and know what this job is about better than anyone else. You might as well get paid for what you're already doing."

I applied and got the job, in which I was basically paid 15 hours per week. Little did I know that four amazing "new" opportunities were about to present themselves in the form of challenges that would change the trajectory of Ashland's Winter Shelter for the near future. More about that in the next few sections!

# Let's Get Started...

What can you expect to find in this book?

Next, you will learn how to customize your own community's solution to homelessness by first discovering how Ashland tailor-made its unique solution by following three (3) simple steps:

1. Humanize
2. Stabilize
3. Self-Actualize

Then, you'll learn to plan for the top three (3) shifts in your community's thinking that happened here in Ashland:

- Mindset Shift 1 - From-Old-to-New-Model
- Mindset Shift 2 - From-Problem-to-Opportunity
- Mindset Shift 3 - From-Silos-to-Community-Partnerships

You'll get a sneak peek into the unique Listening Project.

You're in for a treat when you hear firsthand from a key volunteer who found her fit in Ashland's Winter Shelter. She shares key AHA and WOW moments for her during the last season.

Finally, this book will conclude with a unique "call to action" for you and your community.

Let's get started with customizing your solution to the homeless problem...

# How to Customize Your Solution (3 Steps)

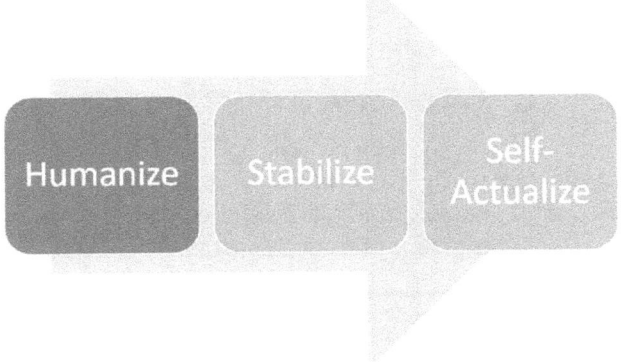

Without a clear path to tailor your own community's unique solutions to the homeless problem, you will likely find yourself lost in a forest of complexity, wondering if you'll ever find a clear, simple path.

What I'm sharing here is a path to self-sufficiency for your unhoused neighbors. In three (3) simple steps, you'll discover how to be more efficient and get more done with less effort by being more strategic on where you focus your and your community's attention and efforts for the greatest results.

Here is Step 1: Humanize...

## Step 1 - Humanize

*"Each one of the people I meet -- you get the outer layers peeled off -- and you discover that there's a real human being there."* ~Buckminster Fuller

Every home-less person is without a home, but not without a name. Their names are Ray or Thomas or Steve or Sally or Grace, etc. Without a name, it's too easy to overlook, misunderstand and pigeonhole each of our neighbors into the same category called "homeless". Big mistake!

I'd like to introduce you to four (4) amazing people -- Matt, Rick, Dale and Wally -- just a few of our unhoused neighbors!

## Story: Finding Gloves for Matt

I'm glad to announce that you don't have to solve the big problem of homelessness all by yourself or all at once! One way to start is by solving the most immediate problem in front of you.

For example, I was walking to Starbucks one morning. I recognized Matt, one of the shelter guests from past seasons, holding a sign.

It was very cold outside. I could see that his hands were turning blue. I blurted, "Hi Matt! Aren't your hands cold? Could you use some gloves?"

He smiled back, "Yes, they're cold. Yes, I could use some gloves."

This became my "mission": **to find gloves for Matt**. I decided that the very next person that I ran into, I was going to tell them about my mission.

I walked down the street a bit. I saw Dale, another shelter guest. He had his red dustpan and broom, sweeping the street.

"Dale," I said. "I'm on a mission to find gloves for Matt. Do you know where I can find some?"

"Here, he can have mine!" he blurted as he started removing his gloves.

"I don't want to take your gloves," I replied with concern.

"Don't worry," he said. "I know where to get some more."

I was touched that he was willing to give away his to another in need.

I turned around and walked half-a-block back to give them to Matt.

Right there, within a matter of minutes and sharing my mission, Dale helped me solve the problem of finding gloves for Matt.

Likewise, solving the BIG problem of homelessness can begin with solving small, immediate problems (small missions) that present themselves, right there in front of your eyes.

I invite you to become willing to solve that very next small or maybe not so small problem for an unhoused neighbor.

Let that be your next "finding gloves for Matt" mission!


## Story: Meet Rick (4th of July Parade 2018)

Some of our unhoused residents are combat veterans. When I heard that veterans could walk in the 4th of July parade in Ashland, I began reaching out to our homeless vets. While most were unavailable, one of the regulars in our winter shelter, Rick, was excited to walk. He had just returned to Ashland after some time away, in time for me to give him a 2018 commemorative 4th of July t-shirt with the One Site logo on the back (thanks to donations from several local residents).

I was surprised and excited to see that he was no longer in a wheelchair. He did not miss a step either. He walked the entire length of the parade route, never complaining, smiling and joking all the way. He was deeply touched by the overwhelming support and appreciation from the crowd that at the end of the parade. Thank you for your service, Rick!

With Rick in the photos below, you'll see City Councilwoman Jackie Bachman, U.S. Senator Ron Wyden, City Councilman Dennis Slattery and other veterans...

## Story: Meet Dale, A Street Angel

I was walking down the steps by Ashland Creek on my usual morning walk. It was early November 2017. With funky music playing in my headphones and my attention on not falling down the steps, I barely noticed the man walking up the steps, sweeping up cigarette butts. It wasn't until we passed each other that I recognized him from last season. I didn't say anything.

Later in front of Starbucks, I took off my headphones and asked, "Dale, what are you doing?"

"I'm bored," he replied, not skipping a beat, sweeping another cigarette butt into his shiny new red, upright standing dust pan. "What a great idea," I beamed. He said he just bought his plastic receptacle to sweep trash. The yard sale folks wanted $18 for the broom which was more than he wanted to pay.

Leaning down and looking closely, I could see the bristles were completely worn down from overuse. I told him I would see if I could find a broom and bring it to him on Sunday night at the shelter.

I was on another mission: to find a broom. First, I thought of my own broom at home which I could loan him until I found another "new" one. I could probably borrow a broom from my landlord if I needed one for my place.

I went home, picked up my broom and loaned it to Dale until I could find another.

Then, I posted the story on Facebook. One of my former students, Sue Swensen, was the first to respond:

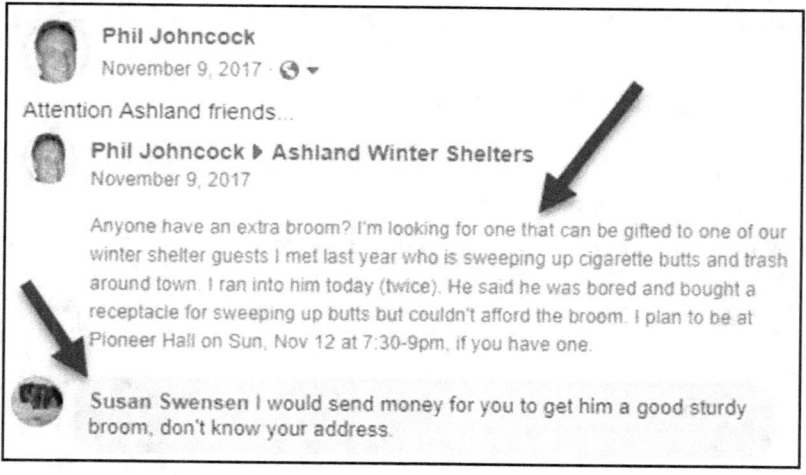

When Sue's generous donation arrived, I walked with Dale to Ace Hardware. We picked up a broom that he liked. Then, we posted a "thank you" video on YouTube. Actually, her donation was more than enough to get another two brooms. It appears that they wear down very fast!

## Story: Meet Wally, An Artist

Wally is a man with many talents. As a musician, he plays the piano and even the harp. Just yesterday, he said he wants to learn how to play the ukulele. I'm sure he will, too! He seems to have a way of doing whatever he sets his mind to.

Photos by Jean-Francous Durand (www.francous.com)

Locally, Wally's known for the beautiful flowers he makes (see the Dedication for the bouquet of flowers he was commissioned to make for me). Making the best of staying warm in the Ashland Public Library, he picked up books on origami. Then, staying at Ashland's Winter Shelter, he began creating colorful flowers, which he still makes and sells today.

Visit Wally's elegant and colorful creations at
**facebook.com/wallace.foreverflowers**.

Wally brings such color and joy to so many!

In a recent Facebook post, he wrote, "Here's a pair of flowers for the obstacles of life today. I hope they put a smile on your face, as they did mine while I made them !!! Have a wonderful evening !!!" Thank you, Wally!

Wally's story was featured in *Ashland Tidings* on January 15, 2019.

## Survey Your Unhoused Neighbors

Another way to get to know your unhoused residents is by interviewing them! This happened in Ashland when we surveyed 57 guests in the 2017-18 winter shelter season. What was amazing was that the survey was actually inspired by Dale, our Street Angel, but not an idea I warmed to right away.

I remember Dale eagerly sharing his experiences of staying at many shelters across the country. He even worked in several programs. He remarked that to get more funding, more accurate data would have to be collected on our guests. While he was right, I did not feel like I had the time (or interest) in putting something together.

My lack of interest did not stop Dale, though. He continued lobbying for a survey at the shelter until some of the hosts and volunteers approached me about his idea. Begrudgingly, I agreed to put together, with Dale's help, a one-page table that could be used to collect data about our shelter guests.

Initially, the survey failed. Several volunteers agreed to interview guests using the form. They returned at the end of the evening with only a very few fields filled out on the form. They said that guests were not really open to answering personal questions about their lives.

I was about ready to give up, when another volunteer, Kacky Hoffman, returned with every single data field in her form filled out. "What did you do differently from these other volunteers?" I asked after showing her the empty forms.

"Basic stuff, actually," she replied. "The first thing I did was tell them my name and a little bit about myself like I had just moved to Ashland. I told them that I wanted to ask questions because we're doing a survey

16

that will help us develop the shelter program better and maybe lead to getting grant money so that we would have more funds for services."

"I always sat down," she continued. "I didn't stand up. I sat down on the floor. I remember the first person I interviewed. I thought, 'Oh, I have to sit on this floor. It's so dirty.' You can't be standing up with the clipboard. You have to be conversational. You have to be right there with them. Of course, you don't look them in the eyes. You look next to the person. There are all these body language things you need to do and be aware of to make them comfortable and trust you and pick up on their cues. Just basic stuff."

While it may be basic stuff for a retired school psychologist like Kacky, for volunteers who've never done it before, it was challenging. It is easy to see why some volunteers returned with empty forms.

"They liked chocolates, too," she chimed. "I brought Hershey's Kisses."

Thankfully, Kacky agreed to take a few more evenings and interview the remaining guests in late December 2017 and early January 2018.

The results of her interviews of 57 guests were significant:

When asked IF they moved to Ashland because of services here, every homeless person said, "No". Likewise, 75% said they became homeless in-state (Oregon) (98% of these local).

Highlights illustrate the severity of the Ashland homeless crisis:

- 54% are disabled.
- The average length of time being homeless is 46.6 months.
- The average age is 44.2. The youngest is 23. The oldest is 72.
- 28% are considered "chronic homeless" (at least 4 years).
- 25% are female.
- 17.5% are veterans.

Many people believe that the homeless should be most interested in getting a job or finding housing. To guests, it's much more immediate like "what's for dinner?" In the freezing cold of winter nights, the biggest challenge they tell us is "getting and staying warm."

Many thanks to Dale who insisted that we collect this valuable data as well as to Kacky who made everyone feel at ease.

## Share Survey Results

Immediately, opportunities presented themselves to share our stories, our local data. By combining accurate statistics about Ashland's unhoused neighbors with their real-life stories, it appeared that many local leaders were beginning to feel the nudge to "step up" to address a problem that previously appeared abstract and muddied. Here are summaries of two specific presentations (a week apart) and two "calls to action" that quickly furthered our community efforts:

1. City Council Presentation (June 4, 2018)
2. Interfaith Social Justice Coalition (June 11, 2018)

## City Council (June 4, 2018)

Heidi asked me to speak with her when she reported to the Ashland City Council on the accomplishments of the 2017-18 winter shelter season. I shared the results of the survey of 57 guests to the Council. One outcome of that specific City Council study session was the decision to form a "working group" to find a location to replace Pioneer Hall for four nights per week of winter shelter starting in November 2018. The Group of 5 was comprised of two councillors (Dennis Slattery and Jackie Bachman), two experience shelter hosts and site coordinators (Vanessa Houk and John Wieczorek) and the Acting City Administrator (Adam Hanks).

The Group of 5 met throughout the summer of 2018. They looked at properties and buildings owned by the City of Ashland, as well as private properties within the city and the Urban Growth Boundary. They frequently met with the One Site Committee to review findings and pursue leads for potential sites. Later in July and August, the group expanded to include additional community partners (i.e., faith-based institutions and nonprofits).

## Interfaith Social Justice Coalition (June 11, 2018)

Sitting outside the circle of attendees, I didn't really have anything planned to say. As I was invited to join the circle, I found myself sharing the results from the interviews of 57 homeless guests. Why? Because it was fresh in my mind.

I didn't know much about the Interfaith Social Justice Coalition, except that it was a collaboration of congregations in Ashland who meet once a month. I learned that they were interested in "dialogue and action toward peace, justice, and environmental sustainability within the Rogue Valley and the wider world."

What I didn't realize was that behind the scenes the Coalition had been considering putting together a "faith summit" in Summer 2018 in Ashland on the issue of "homelessness". After I spoke to the group and answered questions, Rich Rohde began to facilitate a planning session. It was an honor to see the group take the data and run with it. The result was a "faith summit" that took place two months later:

# Voices of Faith for Solutions for Homelessness

A conversation for people of faith.

Please RSVP

offmgr@ashlandmethodist.org
Registration details are at the bottom of the page.

NO ACT OF KINDNESS, NO MATTER HOW SMALL, IS EVER WASTED.

## August 15, 2018 4pm-8:30pm
First United Methodist Church of Ashland

Over 100 people attended the "faith summit." The Coalition did an exceptional job getting out the word to the faith communities and local leaders as well as concerned citizens while creating a program that addressed significant issues around homelessness.

Step one is "humanize". We did that by getting to know each homeless guest and interviewing them. Then, we shared this information with the community.

Step 2 of the process of customizing our community's solution to the homeless problem is "stabilize".

## Step 2 - Stabilize

At the foundation level of Abraham Maslow's Hierarchy of Needs are the basic physical needs of food, clothing and shelter. For our unhoused neighbors to move on to seek to fulfill psychological needs of belongingness, love and esteem, even self-fulfillment including achieving one's full potential, communities must provide a degree of stability (i.e., help them get their basic needs met):

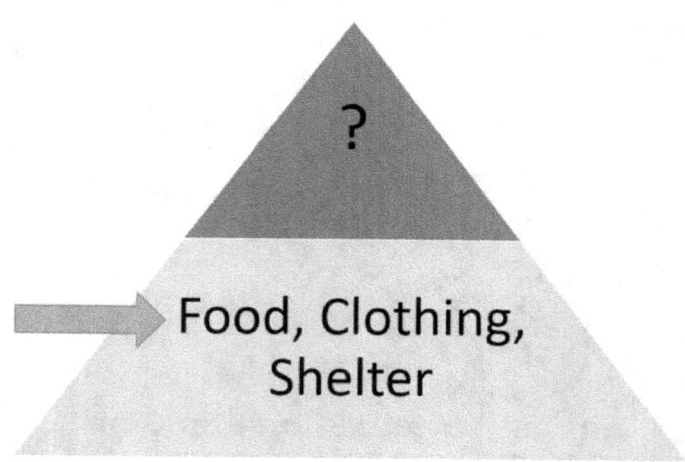

In this section, you will find six (6) examples of local and national programs which address these basic physical needs of food, clothing and shelter.

## Food - Model: Uncle Food's Diner

Recently, I spoke with Elizabeth Hallett, Executive Director of the Peace House, which runs Uncle Food's Diner, a unique one-stop, one-site meal program in Ashland. I asked her about the Diner and how to start one and even write grants! Here is part of our conversation:

Initially, Uncle Food's Diner was just for teenagers who seemed to be homeless or couchsurfing in other people's homes because they weren't feeling safe at home or because they didn't have a home.

It was started by Kevin Priester when he was the director of Peace House. He was a director from 1992 to 1993. He became the director of Peace House following in the footsteps of Selena Aiken. The Gulf War had ended. The peace movement was shifting. We didn't know what the next thing was.

Uncle Food's Diner (UFD) was something that he hit on because Peace House was a nonprofit. We began to look for some money. He created a project around it. Originally, there were maybe 8 to 16 kids, mainly males. They were hungry. The project started actually out of the senior center on Home Street, then moved to Trinity Episcopal and now First United Methodist Church of Ashland which has been doing it now for approximately 14 years.

The UFD meal was held at Trinity Epicopal Church for about 10 years and has been at the Methodist Church for 15.

We have to credit Chris Jones, the Office Manager from the Methodist Church. She's been there for over 30 years. She made the contracts with services that are now part of the Diner experience:

- La Clinica bus (health care)
- "Foot washing" project with the nursing students at Southern Oregon University (SOU)
- Shower trailer with Options for Helping Residents of Ashland (OHRA)
- And, much more!

The program shifted from serving 16 young people to "serving everybody." This happened because hungry people who knew the kids on the street would come and stay outside. They would have the kids go in and get food for them.

I said, "This is ridiculous. We need to open this up to everybody." So, we did. More people started coming. Over the next two years, the program grew to be about 80 people which is about the number we have on our low count. Today, on our most outrageous days, we'll have a hundred and fifty (150) people come to the Diner.

For the last seven or eight years, Leigh Madsen (OHRA) and Rev. Dorita Betts-Borgerson (Methodist church) have provided oversight for the Diner as part of their ministries.

Maren has been the head cook for six years. Peace House writes grants to get funding. Initially, the church gave the building for free until last year. That's all part of the model. The church gave the space. Peace House covers the insurance for the project so that if anything happened to the equipment, the insurance would cover it. For example, there was a fire in an oven. and a dishwasher broke down. We also cover the cost of rug-cleaning 3-4 times per year for Wesley Hall.

The church has provided considerable storage space. They provided an industrial refrigerator. Peace House bought another one with grant money. We have the use of both, sharing them with the church according to our meal and their functions.

Maren is an amazing coordinator for the different food that has to be cooked every Tuesday. She has a strong nucleus of volunteers who are very faithful. One person does the bread pudding. Another one does mashed potatoes. One does salads. One does fruit. And so on.

She's got her own sort of "machine" going by plugging each of those people into production that's really brilliant.

The model also has three different tiers of volunteers or cycles of volunteers. We have the ones that come in around 12 pm. They help cook until 4 pm. There are some people who come in to do set up. We have the ones who serve the food, and that's their thing. Then, we have the people who come in to clean up.

I marvel. Every time I go there on Tuesday, everybody's engaged. It happens out of the goodwill and lack of ego.

Helping other people gives them meaning. We've seen that time and time again.

I am the liaison with the church. I have a great relationship with Chris.

Then, of course we have to deal with NIMBY neighbors like every program that serves this specific population.

Because of some of the issues with neighbors, we ended up having to hire Kip to be security person who is there from 11 am until 7 pm. People start coming sometimes early in the morning but can't use the facilities until 4 pm.

Precautions should be put in place to take care of the building, take care of the neighborhood, take care of the volunteers, and take care of the diner. You need rules to generate the safety. Then, you have to respond to issues that arise. It's inevitable that something will come up."

### *Starting an Uncle Food's Diner*

If your community wanted to start one, the first thing I would do is look for a "location" most likely a church or a synagogue that's willing to work with you. You need a kitchen. You need people who are willing to work with you. The ancient, traditional value of hospitality for all is Biblical and part of many cultural traditions. If there is a community that believes in this and in applying it to the homeless and food insecure, then there is a common value and goal with a Diner Program.

To make it happen, I would say start with a simple meal like soup and sandwiches. Down the road, you can expand to larger meals. Those running the kitchen need to have food handler's licenses-- through a simple on-line class and quiz. OHRA pays for our volunteers to take the quiz. There is a small fee.

You should start looking for volunteers. You should establish a relationship with the health department.

The location ideally needs to have a kitchen that is or can become certified with the health department. The location needs to be accessible to the people you want to serve. The kitchen needs to be maintained to Health Department standard as they will inspect from time to time. We have always gotten a 100% evaluation!

You might want to search for programs in your area like Ashland Food Angels which brings a lot of recycled, yet usable food. According to its website (AshlandFoodAngels.org), "Ashland Food Angels is a grassroots, fully volunteer cooperative venture which helps other organizations serving low income people in the Rogue Valley, primarily through the daily collection and redistribution of food retrieved from markets, bakeries and local organic farmers."

Start small. Start with people from a Beloved Community that wants to work together. They don't have to believe in God. They need to have some common, heart-centered approach or belief system.

Then, there is insurance for your staff and volunteers. People use knives. They're around fire. Things can happen to them or to equipment in the kitchen.

Finding people and faith communities who are "committed" to making a difference is really the first thing. Find a nonprofit under which you can write grants.

### Writing Grants

When you're writing grants, we've found that some funders like to give money to women and children, so you can focus on that in your proposal. They often like to give money to help single parents get back on their feet. We put people in touch with agencies that can help them get jobs and training.

I mention that we feed special populations: low-income people in the community, families, seniors, people with addictions or feeling unwell. I try to give the sense that there's a whole strata of the population that may live in a house, but they are "food insecure." They can't cook for themselves. Perhaps they're too elderly, or they're not well.

I mention that all leftovers are either given to people to take with them for future meals, or they're recycled to another program. Even our scraps are recycled into a farm, as animal feed. There's zero waste.

Funders like it when you're collaborating with other partners in the community. This is really easy for us to say. Because I say that we provide the platform (the meal) for all these other services to happen.

It became a one-stop, one-site service to a whole variety of people in the community who wouldn't otherwise have access to the resources we provide.

Sometimes I'll tell a story about somebody who used to come who now comes back to visit. They're doing better. They've got a job. They're living in a little apartment. They've stabilized. The Diner really helped them through a rough time."

Source: Elizabeth Hallett (Thank you, Elizabeth!)


## Food - Winter Shelter Meals

Heidi Parker is fond of saying that she never had to focus on food during her 6-year tenure coordinating Ashland's Winter Shelter. "Food just shows up," she used to say, speaking to how meals magically appeared.

In the 2018-19 season, it was our community's night sponsors, night coordinators and hundreds of volunteers who made sure we had meals seven-nights-a-week at the winter shelter:

- Sunday: South Mountain Friends Meeting (Quakers)
- Monday: First Presbyterian Church
- Tuesday: Temple Emek Shalom
- Wednesday: Trinity Episcopal
- Thursday: Rogue Valley Unitarian Universalist Fellowship
- Friday: United Congregational Church of Christ
- Saturday: Southern Oregon Jobs With Justice

It helped that the community offered daily meals as well in the afternoon: Komac on Sundays; Vanessa/Jason Houk and Lisa Ostos on Mondays,

Wednesdays, Thursdays, Fridays and Saturdays; and Peace House and Uncle Food's Diner on Tuesdays. Many of our shelter guests attended these meals in the afternoon, even helped out on many occasions. Of course, it took hundreds of volunteers to pull off meals seven-days-a-week. Thank you to all who fed the entire community!

By the time guests entered the shelter at 7:30 pm, many had had a warm meal. However, many did not. For some, they were hungry again having burned off a lot of calories out in the cold and walking across town from Pioneer Hall (downtown) to Presbyterian church (site for the shelter on Fridays, Saturdays and Sundays).

## Clothing - Model: Laundry Love

According to the National Laundry Love website (LaundryLove.org), "The story of Laundry Love began in 2003 with T-Bone (Eric), a houseless gentleman living in Ventura, CA. In one particular conversation, a question was asked of him: "How can we come alongside your life in a meaningful way?" His response was honest and practical. "If I had clean clothes I think people would treat me like a human being."

"The Laundry Love initiative consists of regular opportunities to come alongside people who are struggling financially by assisting them with their laundry. Laundry Love partners with groups and local laundromats in cleaning clothes and linens for low-income or no-income families and individuals. We see the laundromat as a place where strangers become friends, people are known by name, and the worth of every human being is acknowledged and celebrated."

You can find a Laundry Love program near you (or even start one) by visiting the website: LaundryLove.org. Over 1,300,000 loads of laundry and more than 950,000 people have been served since 2003 with an estimated 72,000 individuals cared for annually.

### Locally (In Ashland)

In the summer of 2015, the newly formed Local Justice and Witness Committee of the Ashland United Church of Christ (UCC) was searching for a meaningful way for the congregation to support the community. At the suggestion of Dee Anne Everson, church member and Executive Director of United Way, the Committee chaired by Hedy Schoonover and Alexandra Reid researched and then initiated a local Laundry Love program by approaching Nick Baida, owner of Henry's Laundromat. Fortunately, Nick was familiar with the Laundry Love concept because volunteers at his laundromat in Grants Pass were already providing Laundry Love services. We began providing Laundry Love in Ashland in October 2015.

Members of the Committee started raising funds for Laundry Love by putting out a donation jar in the church's fellowship hall. As time went by, fundraising has expanded to include grants from the national UCC, United Way, local foundations, local businesses, other local congregations, regular individual donors and an annual fundraising event to come up with the necessary $6,000-a-year to run the program. Laundry detergent and other laundry aids are also donated, along with clean clothes to offer guests who need something to wear as they wash everything they own.

Laundry Love is currently available in Ashland on the 2nd Saturday of every month from 1-4 pm at Henry's Laundromat. Six-to-eight volunteers divide the afternoon into two shifts during which we offer quarters for the machines and honest friendship to everyone who comes in the door. We spend between $300 and $650 during the afternoon as our 40-50 guests fill every machine with their clothing and bedding. We figure out together how best to use the machines, offer to help our guests fold their laundry, play with their children, providing them with books and art supplies, admire the dogs, visit with new acquaintances and long-time friends and listen to one another's stories.

As T-Bone prophesied, people are treated like human beings when their clothes are clean. They have more dignity and self-respect. Guests seem to feel calmer and more relaxed as they depart the laundromat. There is a little more order in their difficult lives. We all have enjoyed an afternoon of positive social interaction. One young man nodded and grinned at me on his way out last month. "You've got a good vibe going on in here," he said.

Source: Alex Reid (Thanks, Alex!)

## Clothing & Shower - Pre-Shelter Orientation

Before our winter shelter season that started on November 11, 2018, we tried something unique. We set it up as an "orientation day" prior to the beginning of the winter shelter. A shower trailer was set up for people to come in and take a shower, as well as clothes and volunteers to welcome prospective guests.

Clothes were donated. We purchased different sizes of underwear and bras for everyone.

We contacted people who were pre-screened to let them know about the special event.

When pre-screened individuals arrived, they would put their name on the schedule for a shower. Then, they came upstairs at the United Methodist Church of Ashland and picked out some clothes. Then, they took a shower, put old clothes in a bag and put on new clothes they just picked out.

With a shower and clean set of clothes, they met with someone from our team. They were given the Guest Agreement Form (Appendix C), which they signed. There were asked if they had six (6) essential services: health insurance, ID, SNAP food stamps, phone, bus pass and mailbox.

If guests indicated they did not have a specific essential service, they were asked if they were interested in acquiring it. If "yes", they were asked if they would like our help.

Laundry Love agreed to take dirty clothes, wash them and bring them to the first evening of shelter. Thank you! Laundry Love, both the national and local programs, are described above.

Guests were given a paper with the locations of the shelter.

This was a great way to start out the season. Everybody was clean. Everyone had a chance to get some new clothes and be welcomed into the family.

On the next page is a photo of Henry Knutsen and Grant Williams, two volunteers who ran the shower trailer, loaned by Grayback Forestry Inc and managed by Leigh Madsen and OHRA:

## Clothing: Showers & Laundry - Model: Dignity on Wheels

Dignity on Wheels is a model shower and laundry program. Since launching in September 2015 (and through January 2017), their results have been impressive:

- 1,484 – Number of unduplicated individuals to receive services
- 4,803 – Number of hot showers provided
- 1,680 – Number of single loads of laundry provided

According to the Dignity on Wheels website (DignityOnWheels.org), "the lack of showers and toilets is a growing and critical problem for the homeless, and a key reason many do not seek employment, housing assistance or other social services for which they are eligible. This is a reflection of how American society continues to marginalize, discriminate against and sometimes criminalize the homeless, and this is especially prevalent in Silicon Valley."

They often, "suffer the indignity of traveling on public transportation in an unclean state.

Mobile shower buses and trailers are emerging and are providing a much needed service to the homeless. However, many of the programs lack proper 1) logistical execution, 2) financial sustainability 3) community buy-in and support, and 4) long-term lasting results for homeless individuals rebuilding their lives and getting off the street."

"Dignity on Wheels provides free showers, toilets, and laundry services to homeless and at risk individuals in the San Mateo County community," partnering "with NPOs, FPOs, Faith-based organizations, local and county government agencies, and community centers who may already have an outreach program with homeless or at-risk clientele."

"Our trailer arrives about 30 minutes before the scheduled session to set-up and handle any unforeseen obstacles. We have up to 3 staff members accompany the trailer to the site. Clients arrive intermittently and are served on a first come first served basis. We gather basic demographic data. If the client wants to take a shower, they are issued a towel and a shower room."

"Clients are allowed 15 minutes in the shower room with 7 minutes of hot water. If the client wants to wash some clothes, we issue them a mesh bag to put their clothes in. Laundry takes about an hour to complete. Once a client is finished taking a shower or with their laundry, they leave the premises."

They have "not had any issues with loitering. Usually our clients come and conduct business and leave. There are times when clients need to wait for laundry to finish or for a partner to shower. Our experience has been that they wait quietly, pass the time, converse with a fellow client, or conduct other business elsewhere and return at a later time to pick up clothing or partners."

If there are disruptive clients, "our staff is trained in conflict resolution and de-escalation techniques. In our 18 months of business we have had two incidents of disruption. In each instance our staff could de-escalate the situation and restore the session normalcy quickly."

For more information, visit DignityOnWheels.org.

### Locally (In Ashland)

Locally, while a customized shower trailer (with laundry services) was being readied for use in Ashland, Grayback Forestry Inc loaned Options for Helping Residents of Ashland (OHRA) its shower trailer in FY 2018-

19. The shower trailer was made available on Tuesdays at Ashland's First United Methodist Church (Uncle Food's Diner) and Saturdays at The Grove. At this moment, OHRA's tailor-made shower trailer is available! Many thanks to Leigh Madsen for managing the shower trailer!

## Shelter - Winter Shelter

Ashland's Winter Shelter is an emergency shelter for homeless that runs during the coldest months of the year (November 1 through March 31). Up to forty-six (46) pre-screened and approved guests with bed reservations for the 2019-20 season may arrive at the shelter after 6 pm and depart by 10 am.

Transportation (a mini-bus) will be provided to/from the shelter and to/from educational programs and services at the shelter and other locations in Jackson County designed to help chronic homeless, homeless vets and the most vulnerable homeless residents move along the Continuum of Care towards self-sufficiency.

Case management (i.e., housing and job search, essential services, etc.) will be provided during the shelter season and year-round to provide immediate and long-term solutions.

Data collection services begins with a Service Prioritization Decision Assistance Tool (SPDAT) individual screening off-site at the Ashland Community Resource Center with results entered into Service Point to activate Coordinated Entry Services county-wide.

Separately, an Extreme Weather Warming Center will be offered at other locations in Ashland when temperatures drop to 20 degrees or below.

Program (or operations) state grant funds cover expenses such as water, cleaning, laundry, office supplies, storage, rent/utilities, septic tank pumping, transportation, HMIS licensing, WiFi, training (bringing the Built for Zero model to the community). Staff expenses include a bookkeeper, coordinator, data collection, Extreme Weather Warming Center, fire watch, case management (on-site and off-site), experienced overnight hosts, shuttle drivers, SPDAT screening and support.

Step 2 is "stabilize". We stabilized by providing food, clothing and shelter during the coldest months of the year (November through March).

Step 3 of the process of customizing the community's solution to the homeless problem is "self-actualize," which means helping to "realize" one's true potential.

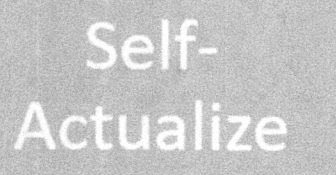

# Step 3 - Self-Actualize

Once you have a roof over your head and a bed-for-a-season, then what?

In the mid 1980s, across the U.S., "self-sufficiency" became a goal for the homeless along a path of realizing their true potential. It was used by many funding sources and human service programs for the homeless.

What does it mean to be self-sufficient? Let's see as we move down the path to self-sufficiency...

***Path of Self-Sufficiency***

The intent of the "new" model of Ashland's Winter Shelter -- beyond getting a good night's sleep -- was to provide immediate and long-term solutions to our community's chronic, veteran and most vulnerable homeless on a path toward self-sufficiency along a Continuum of Care (explained later).

In order to achieve self-sufficiency and economic security, we first assessed their immediate needs for six (6) essential services (i.e., health insurance, IDs, phones, SNAP food stamps, mailbox, bus pass) on the first night of shelter. Then, we began to access more long-term needs by employing a self-sufficiency matrix in multiple areas of their lives which is a federally-approved assessment and accountability measurement tool.

The result of the assessment was an individualized roadmap from "crisis" of immediate need to temporary support "stability" on a path to self-sufficiency using nine (9) primary categories:

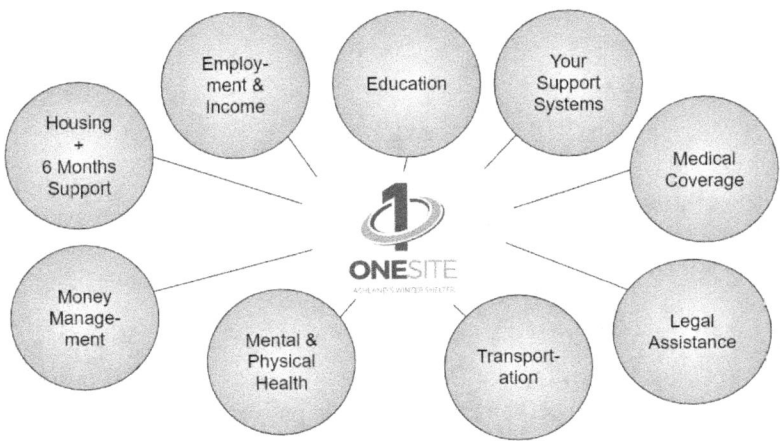

We selected these as the most important nine (9) key areas on which to focus our efforts first and foremost with the homeless in Ashland. These come from a larger list developed in the 1990s by Dr. Diana Pearce, a researcher and professor at the University of Washington. She developed a Self-Sufficiency Standard, a measure of "income adequacy" now used in thirty-seven (37) states.

Dr. Pearce's Standard defines "self-sufficiency" in twenty-five (25) key areas or "outcome scales":

Access to Services
Career Resiliency/Training
Childcare
Clothing
Education
Employment
English Language Skills
Food
Functional Ability
Housing
Income (Self-Sufficiency Standard)
Income (Area Median Income)
Income (Federal Poverty Level)

Legal
Life Skills (Household Management)
Life Skills (Human Resources)
Life Skills (Financial Matters)
Life Skills (Setting Goals & Resourcefulness)
Mental Health
Parenting
Physical Health
Safety
Substance Use
Support Systems
Transportation

Based on Dr. Pearce's work, a Self-Sufficiency Matrix was developed to measure the progress of individuals moving in each key area (identified by each unique program) from "in-crisis" to "self-sufficient" and even "thriving":

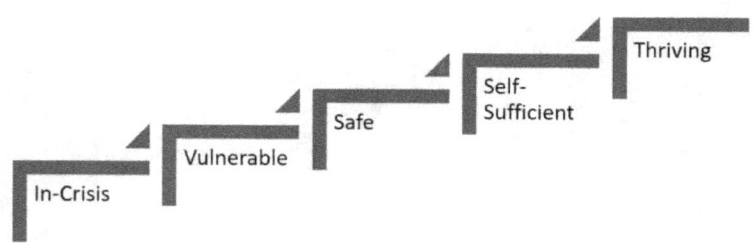

Let's look at an example: the category of "transportation". When most homeless come to us, they are "in-crisis" without a way to get around. Few have their own cars. We purchased bus passes, which they could use to get to places where they could also secure benefits, search for jobs, make and keep appointments, seek healthcare, look for housing, go to work, access showers and meals, go to AA meetings, counseling, and more.

As a result of having bus passes, guests progress quickly from level 1 (in-crisis) to level 4 (self-sufficient). Likewise, by helping them get full medical coverage, guests moved from "in-crisis" to "self-sufficient" fast!

Now, here's the amazing thing...

The positive impact of moving up levels is uplifting, too! Just by experiencing and observing others movements from "in-crisis" to "self-sufficient" in one or more specific areas of their lives was more than often enough to inspire others around them to also pursue improving conditions in their lives. For example, guests shared that they began quitting smoking and drinking, applied for college, got a job, sought legal assistance, developed support systems, and much more!

It was as if the experience of upward movement in one or more areas sparked something inside (including self-confidence) which in turn inspired many guests to want to realize their potential in other areas of their lives. Wow! What a joy it is to witness this happen. The self-esteem from taking baby steps and achieving small and big goals in a supportive community was beautiful to witness and be part of!

Photos by Jean-Francóus Durand (www.francous.com)

Step 3 is "self-actualize". We helped stabilized winter shelter guests move along a path of self-sufficiency.

With these 3 steps in place, let's now explore three (3) community mindsets that shifted...

# Mindset Shift 1
# From-Old-to-New-Model

*"Innovation and best practices can be sown throughout an organization - but only when they fall on fertile ground."*
~Marcus Buckinham, British Author

Mindset Shift 1 empowered the Ashland community to embrace a new "model" to take our winter shelter to the next level. Here is how it worked...

## Model Programs

During its first ten seasons (starting in 2008), Ashland's Winter Shelter primarily focused on providing "direct 'no frills' services" and related services (i.e., food, clothing, etc.) starting with shelter on one night and then expanding to six nights.

The 2018-19 (11th) winter season served as a unique opportunity to 1) identify and put into effect "model" practices from other shelters and 2) make a successful transition from a "drop in" shelter on a "first-come, first-served" basis to a "pre-screened" mode in which guests have a-bed-for-a-season (5 months).

## Comparing Old with New

To start, it was important to define the difference between the "old" model of what we had and the "new" model vision that we wanted to create.

Here is a comparison table of the old and new models:

| 2017-18 (Old Model) | 2018-19 (New Model) |
|---|---|
| 4-6 nights | 7 nights |
| 3 sites | 4 sites (until One Site is approved & ready) |
| No frills (mats) | Optimal sleeping with cots & storage (at One Site) |
| 1st come, 1st served (drop in) | Bed-for-a-season (or until housed) \| Pre-screening with most vulnerable given priority for admission |
| No transportation | Bus passes given to all guests (transportation to/from at One Site) |
| Informal case management (if any) | On-site and off-site, year-round case management |
| Daily sign ins | Attendance sheets and outcome/exit reporting |
| No or minimum Continuum of Care | Part of Continuum of Care system in Jackson County |

Of course, there are many "best practice" examples out there. In fact, many effective practices in other communities in Oregon have been identified by experienced volunteers including Heidi and Bob Morse. Heidi shared a national program called "Built for Zero" and spoke frequently of several shelters she had visited in Oregon, California, Canada, etc. Bob scheduled a trip for five of us to travel to Eugene, Oregon, to visit Opportunity Village and meet with community leaders.

Since we had no credibility with running a shelter with the new model, I reached out to others in Jackson County who knew more than I, experts who could speak to the "new" model better than I.

# Orientation: Introducing the "New" Model

On November 8, 2018, we held our usual pre-season Orientation for volunteers. With the recruitment help of David Wick and the Ashland Culture of Peace Commission (ACPC), one of our twelve community partners, we had "standing room only" with 134 volunteers in attendance (a 223% increase in attendance from the previous year).

At the Orientation, in order to help our Ashland community understand the "new" model, I asked Connie Wilkerson, Director of Continuum of Care in Jackson County, to introduce two important concepts: "coordinated entry" and "continuum of care." Both are part of the new model. She brought a great deal of credibility and experience.

In addition, I invited Brandie Barnes, an experienced Case Manager from the Kelly Shelter in neighboring Medford, Oregon, to describe how their second year with a "bed-for-a-season" was remarkably improved from their "drop in" first year when they received quite a few complaints.

Photo at Orientation by Helga Motley (www.helgasplayhouse.com)

One AHA moment came for me a few weeks after the Orientation when someone in our community posted a strong opinion against the "new" model on the Ashland Peeps Facebook page. It was actually an attendee from the Orientation who was one of the first to post a response to clarify and share accurate information about the new model.

39

*"I confess that I was one of the 'doubters' about the new process you brought in. I'm now a believer."* ~Carol Voisin

# "Continuum of Care" Model

In July 2018, our first two homeless neighbors got screened. Immediately, they were placed into housing!

Wow! That was fast!

The first got placed into Hope Village in Medford, Oregon. The second was placed into a home for veterans in Central Point, Oregon.

I knew our new model was good. I never expected 100% placement into housing! How did this happen?

It was a direct benefit of our being part of the Continuum of Care system for Jackson County coordinated by Connie Wilkerson. As a result of getting folks into the Homeless Management Information System (HMIS), case workers from other agencies in the system through the county could access people who had been screened and then place them into housing! Thank you!

### Systems-within-the-System

Luckily, the Continuum of Care program in Jackson County already had two systems-within-the-system in place that we could plug into immediately:

- SPDAT - We used the Service Prioritization Decision Assistance Tool (SPDAT) to screen our unhoused residents. Results were entered into the ServicePoint and HMIS database to activate Coordinated Entry Services county-wide. Once an individual is pre-screened, a support system for immediate need essential services and long-term self-sufficiency support kicked in.
- ServicePoint & HMIS - According to the Homeless Leadership Coalition, "The state of Oregon has instituted ServicePoint to be

the platform for ... data collection. The mission of HMIS is to be an integrated network of homeless, prevention and other service providers that use a central database to collect, track and report uniform information on client needs and services. This system not only meets Federal and State requirements, but also enhances service planning and delivery. Communities can use this information to determine how services are being utilized, identify gaps in the local service continuum and develop outcome measurements."

## Background

According to Oregon Health and Human Services, "the Continuum of Care (CoC) Program originates from the federal Housing and Urban Development (HUD) Agency. The CoC program is designed to promote community-wide commitment to the goal of ending homelessness; provide funding for efforts by nonprofit providers, and State and local governments to quickly rehouse homeless individuals and families while minimizing the trauma and dislocation caused to homeless individuals, families, and communities by homelessness; promote access to and effect utilization of mainstream programs by homeless individuals and families; and optimize self-sufficiency among individuals and families experiencing homelessness."

# "Kelly Shelter" Model

When I first heard about the Kelly Shelter in Medford, Oregon, I had heard that it had just wrapped up a successful second season of winter shelter at the end of March 2018. Its first season was a "first-come, first-served," "drop in" shelter. There were many complaints from neighboring businesses.

For the second season, they switched to a pre-screened model in which the unhoused would have a bed for the 90-day season.

What they discovered in the new pre-screened model was truly amazing. Some neighbors didn't even know they had their shelter there for the first few weeks. They didn't have as many police calls. It was much easier to manage. Leaders realized that it was a smart move. With that experience in mind, I invited Brandie Barnes, the case manager, to come to the Orientation to talk about the first year experience and how that was as the "old" model. Congratulations!

Then I asked her to share her experience with their "new" model in the second year. They also had case management in their second year. Out of 50 people who were guests at the shelter, 40 of them got into housing. That's quite significant. That's an 80% success rate!

The Kelly Shelter was also part of the Continuum of Care system.

In Appendix B, you will find a letter from Brandie. In their 2nd year, she actually witnessed a decrease in crime and an increase in both personal responsibility and respectful attitudes!

In the next section (Mindset Shift 2), we'll explore how we shifted our focus to see problems as opportunities for creative solutions.

# Mindset Shift 2
# From-Problem-To-Opportunity

*"Every problem is an opportunity in disguise."* ~John Adams

Mindset Shift 2 invites us to discover the unique opportunity hidden within each problem, many which seemed impossible to solve initially. Here are nine opportunities that we found:

## Opportunity 1: Not In My Back Yard (NIMBY)

Everyone has an idea around where to house the homeless. For example, take George Carlin in one of his comedy routines:

"I'll tell you what to do about homelessness. First thing, change the name of it. Change the name of the condition. It's not 'homelessness'. It's 'houselessness'. It's houses these people need. A home is an abstract idea. A home is a setting. It's a state of mind. These people need houses, physical, tangible structures.

Where are you gonna build them? Nobody wants you to build low-cost housing near their houses. People don't want it near them. We got something this country you've heard of called NIMBY (Not In My Back Yard). People don't want any kind of social help located anywhere near them.

I got just the place for low-cost housing. I know where we can build housing for the homeless: golf courses! Just what we need... plenty of good land in nice neighborhoods, land that is currently being wasted on a meaningless, mindless activity engaged in primarily by white well-to-do, male businessmen who use the game to get together to make deals to carve this country up a little finer among themselves.

There are over 17,000 golf courses in America they average over 150 acres a piece. That's over 3 million acres. That's four thousand eight hundred and twenty square miles. We could build two Rhode Islands and a Delaware for the homeless..."

When you work with the homeless, NIMBY -- "Not In My Back Yard" -- comes up a lot. It can describe a person or an attitude. A NIMBY might agree that a community or even a neighborhood needs a homeless shelter for unhoused residents trying to get back on their feet, but doesn't want it close to their house.

Locally, it even appeared in the City of Medford's Homeless System Action Plan (April 2019):

- "Political pressures are a factor in the new momentum to address homelessness, both on the part of NIMBY groups as well as locals wanting the City to do something about the issue." (page 59)
- "Strong consensus that a year-round shelter is needed. Difficult to identify a suitable site, for technical reasons as well as NIMBYism." (page 59)

# Opportunity 2: Shift from Liabilities to Assets

I remember my first meeting with Chad McComas, Executive Director of Rogue Retreat. Rogue Retreat is the sister nonprofit of OHRA which runs the winter shelter -- Kelly Shelter -- in the neighboring city in Medford, Oregon. Chad said something truly amazing:

"The average homeless person," he stated proudly, "visits the emergency room of a hospital an average of four times per year, at the cost of $1,000 to $1,500 or more per visit. By providing winter shelter, the number of visits are reduced by almost 50%, a savings of more than $100,000 a year!"

| Average Emergency Visits to Hospital for the Homeless ||
| --- | --- |
| **WITHOUT** SHELTER<br>(4 emergency visits/year)<br>Cost =<br>$100,000+ | **WITH** SHELTER<br>(2 or less emergency visits/year)<br>Savings =<br>$100,000+ |

As important as the financial savings are to local hospitals is the fact that a "before/after" image was indelibly painted in my mind. I began to wonder how winter shelter programs could actually help communities shift their economic mindsets from viewing our homeless neighbors as "liabilities" (costing them over $100,000 per year) to becoming "assets" for our communities (saving them over $100,000 per year).

# Opportunity 3: Valuing Volunteers

For 10 years, volunteers, faith-based groups, nonprofits and government agencies had "showed up" and "stepped up" to offer winter shelter at different locations in Ashland. The degree of volunteerism in this small town is truly inspiring. However, its impact was not fully understood.

One of the first suggestions I made was to assign a financial value to volunteer time. The problem was that there were no timesheets. Yet, there were many jobs performed by volunteers, too:

- Two overnight hosts spent at least 12 hours per night (like 7pm to 7am).
- Kitchen crews worked at least two hours per night (7-9pm).
- Listeners work as many as two hours per night (7-9pm).
- Clean up crews (or co-hosts when no one showed up) worked 1+ hours per morning.

This meant that on any given night of winter shelter, volunteers likely donated at least 29 hours. For a month, that meant at least 870 hours. The problem is that this is an "estimate" and not "accurate", unless actual timesheets were kept. The solution was "keep timesheets."

That is what we did! From the start of the 2018-19 winter shelter season, volunteers at four different venues were asked to "time in" when they arrived and "time out" before they left. Then, total hours were entered daily into a spreadsheet.

The results were quite spectacular, too:

# 5,959 Hours
# 1,242 Volunteer Jobs
## From 11/11/18 to 4/13/19!

Then, when these volunteer hours are assigned a "fair market value," the "actual" monetary value is even more impressive:

# Volunteer Value = $151,041
## (60% increase from 2017-18)

Of course, volunteers are not actually "paid" but rather assigned a monetary equivalency. This is called an "in-kind" donation of goods and services by nonprofit agencies.

At communication opportunities like presentations and eBlasts, I liked to include the actual value of volunteer time to-date. It showed "buy in," the community's acceptance of and willingness to actively support and participate in the project.

Financially, a fair-market value of volunteer time can also be included in internal and external financial statements used by nonprofit businesses as "in-kind support," an alternative and addition to financial contributions (money). It is a donation of goods or services that an organization would have purchased if they had not been donated.

According to the Financial Accounting Standards Board (FASB), the actual value of volunteer time can be used in financial statements such as a nonprofit's Profit & Loss Statements and the Form 990, as well as grant proposals, annual reports, etc. Over four decades, I've learned the benefit of leveraging in-kind donations for programs to request and receive grant funding for items that we couldn't get donated. Funders love to see this level of community buy-in as one indication that they do not have to pay for everything!

"Keeping timesheets" is key! For 40 years, I've kept timesheets for more than 500 jobs that I've had. I "time in" when I start working on each and every project. I "time out" when I stop. It's an ongoing habit that has become part of my everyday routine. It helps keep projects separate for budgeting and manage my time more effectively. I even got $20,000 from a client as a result of keeping a timesheet for additional work performed.

As important as the financial value of volunteer time is verbal and in-writing appreciations of volunteers on a regular basis. This is something in which Heidi Parker excelled. Volunteers also often remark how appreciative they are when a shelter guest genuinely says, "Thank you!"

Here is a group photo taken of our amazing volunteers (including our youngest volunteer at the age of 5) at the Volunteer Appreciation Party for the 2018-19 season:

# Opportunity 4: Community Funds & More In-Kind Donations

One problem that we faced was that no one wanted to pay for inside sprinklers for the Rogue Valley Church (One Site), especially if the building was only going to be used for no more than three years. This shifted into an opportunity when John Noscoe, an OHRA Board member, pointed out the selling-point: the cost of installing sprinklers literally pays for itself. How so?

Without inside sprinklers, we are required by local fire authorities to hire a Fire Watch Coordinator to perform constant patrols (every 15 minutes or so) of the church. It just so happens that the cost of hiring a fire watch position for one year is the same as that of installing sprinklers!

In other words, by installing sprinklers, we would save money by not having to hire a Fire Watch Coordinator for one year. If the church had sprinklers and was used for three years, the savings will be $66,000.

Unfortunately, state grant funding could not be used to pay for sprinklers. So, I put the cost estimate into "community fund" budget along with other expenses that would not be covered by state funds: Type 2 application ($1,700), building repairs, kitchen appliances, mini-bus, etc.

You never know where the funding might come from, and this happened in each of the "community fund" cases. First, it was City Councillor Dennis Slattery who introduced me to Amy Cuddy with the Oregon Community Foundation. Within a few days, I was giving her a tour of the Rogue Valley Church and explaining the cost benefits of getting sprinklers. Within a week, I received an email (November 8, 2018), from Amy stating that her board had met and approved a $25,000 grant for sprinklers.

Second, the Type 2 application fee ($1,700) was gratefully picked up by Reverend Dan Fowler and the First Presbyterian Church of Ashland, a major contributor and community partner!

Third, many building repairs were picked by Ashland Lions Club (special thanks to Pete Jorgenson, Don Johnson and members), Peter McBennett, Henry Knutson and private donors.

The Ashland Lions Club replaced a kicked-in door:

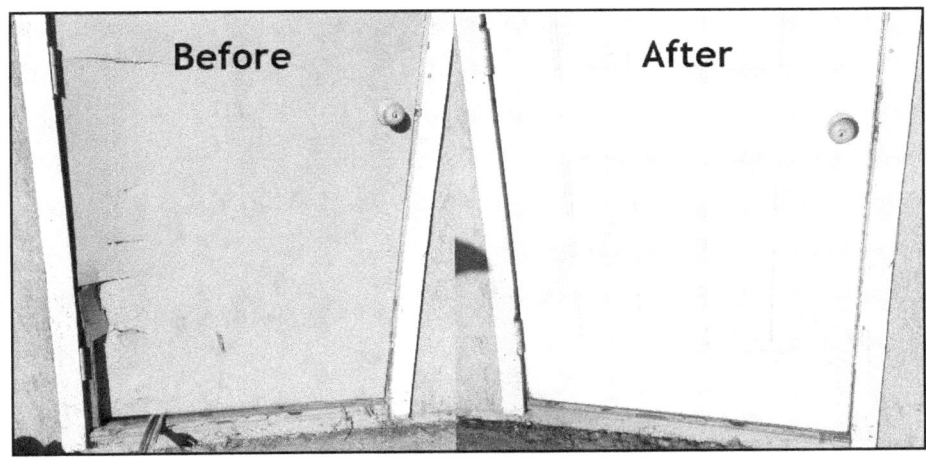

The Ashland Lions Club also installed smoke detectors and carbon monoxide alarms as well as dry-walled the utility closet (a requirement from the Fire District 5 inspection):

They removed bushes outside windows (another Fire District 5 requirement):

Peter McBennett, a valued (and very funny) shelter host and Night Coordinator, painted several walls, hauled away trash, repaired roof tiles, installed exit signs, and so much more!

Henry Knutson unpacked chairs, installed thermostat covers, installed and transferred cots (with help from other volunteers) from Presbyterian to Rogue Valley Church, etc.

Fourth, kitchen appliances (refrigerator, stove, microwave), dishes, cupboard papering, cleaning as well as washer and dryer were purchased by Kim Blackwolf and Trinity Episcopal church.

Fifth, a private donor picked up the cost of purchasing a mini-bus, registration, insurance and decals (plus installation) of One Site name and logos. See story below.

Thank you, everyone!

Overall, community funding represented 58% of the shelter budget.

# Opportunity 5: Mini-Bus

Colleagues and friends often present the most interesting and unique opportunities that are worth considering and acting on. One example was a mini-bus. I was having a meeting with Leo Gorcey. He was telling me about the bus that a local nonprofit was converting into a home for family. He mentioned that they got the bus donated from the Ashland School District (ASD).

A light bulb went off inside. I asked Leo if ASD would be willing to donate a bus for us for One Site to be able to take people to and from the shelter. "I don't know," he replied. "Let's find out."

We hopped into Leo's car. He drove me directly to the ASD Transportation Department to speak with Stacey Delgado, Transportation Director. She didn't have any busses available. Instead, she showed us two mini-buses were going to be auctioned soon on CraigsList. We could get one if we had the winning bid.

Synchronistically, we just happened to receive a generous donation from a private donor to not only make a winning bid for one of the well-maintained vehicles, but to cover the cost for the license and registration, insurance and decals for one mini-bus:

Purchasing the mini-bus would not have happened unless Leo had told me about his unique program and then taken the initiative to introduce me to Stacey.

Thank you, Leo and Stacey.

# Opportunity 6: Expanding the Grant Budget

The City of Ashland has a resolution that when the temperature drops below 20 degrees, an "emergency" declaration for a "drop in" warming center has to be made by the city.

In the past, the City of Ashland had picked up the costs of the "emergency" or extreme weather warming center. The city paid Options for Helping Residents of Ashland (OHRA) to hire overnight hosts and coordinate efforts.

I was impressed with Kelly Madding, the new City Administrator, who had established such great connections with the state funder (ACCESS) that would ultimately lead OHRA and me to renegotiate our state funding budget to cover the costs for additional nights required for an Extreme Weather Warming Center. Kelly made the initial contact with ACCESS that made my job easier. Thanks, Kelly!

I saw this renegotiation of the budget as an opportunity to request additional state funds for rapidly expanding expenses for running a shelter at four different church sites seven-nights-a-week, an additional "emergency" shelter if declared, as well as preparing the Rogue Valley Church for occupancy (once the Type 2 application was approved by Jackson County). Many thanks to the OHRA board for the timely approval of the 9th revised budget.

We requested additional expenses such as "emergency" shelter hosts, year-round case management, fire watch coordination (required by Ashland's Fire Marshall at the three churches without sprinklers), rent and utilities of the Rogue Valley Church, screening and data management, cots, office supplies, cleaning supplies, blankets and washing, food, etc.

Many thanks to Pam Norr and ACCESS, another valued community partner, for making the process of renegotiating the budget easy and pain-free.

# Opportunity 7: Water Table

We had not realized the extent of the water problem at One Site until a neighbor reminded us that the building (Rogue Valley Church) did not use the city's water system. The property is in what is called the Urban Growth Boundary. The building's water comes from a well dug on the property. We knew that.

What we didn't know, but our neighbor pointed out, was that the usage of water on one's property in the county affects the groundwater levels of others in the area. We discovered that a different neighbor had dug a deeper well, which impacted everyone's water table around them. Having 46 guests staying at the shelter every day will definitely require significant usage of water in 5 months. The impact on neighbor's wells will indeed be great!

I thought this new knowledge would be the prophetic straw that broke the camel's back. It might just keep us from getting the approval from Jackson County to use the church for a winter shelter. At least, that's what I thought.

Then, a miracle happened. In speaking with Pam Norr (ACCESS) about revising our shelter grant budget, I shared the bad news. "I don't know what we can do," I said in frustration.

To my amazement, Pam blurted a solution, "Well, you can bring in big tank trucks of water. Our state grant funding could cover it, too!" Wow!

At first, I couldn't picture it. It didn't settle inside as a realistic solution. I'd never brought in water like this. Over time, the idea began to settle in. Then, I wondered, "Where do we store the water?"

I did a little research. There were trucks that could bring in 5,000 gallons of water. There were also 6,000 gallon tanks that we could place on both sides of the building for storing the water. Water from the tanks could be used for multiple purposes, too. In addition to usage in sinks and toilets, it could be used internally for sprinklers and even externally by fire trucks, in case of a fire.

Wow! This idea -- trucking in water and storing it in two tanks at both ends of the building -- could actually work! Costs were put into the FY 2019-21 budget proposal!

# Opportunity 8: Scabies Scare

Sometimes, there are very frightening things that happen that require you to take immediate action. One of these came when several guests arrived at the shelter very upset, claiming that multiple people in the shelter now had scabies. SCABIES! I don't know if you know what that is, but it's scary, especially when people don't understand what it is and isn't.

Basically, scabies is a skin condition. Scabies mites are tiny, insect-like parasites that infect the top layer of the skin. The infection causes rashes, irritation and lots of itching. It can spread to others during skin-to-skin touching.

Sometimes, it hits homeless communities where people are staying in close proximity to each other, especially when they're not able to shower and not able to wash or clean all of their stuff.

We did have some excellent, pre-season training around communicative diseases like scabies, head lice and TB with Gwen Reen from Rogue Community Health.

Nothing prepared us for our reactions when we heard the news of multiple guests potentially with scabies that evening. We freaked out. Everybody was scared.

Before we let guests into the shelter that evening, we convened an emergency meeting of the staff. Several of the volunteers and I sat down to discuss how we should address this issue "before" we allowed guests to enter for the evening.

After some discussion, we decided that instead of allowing people to come in as a group in the front entrance, we would bring people one-by-one in through the back entrance. In this way, we would talk to individuals about what scabies was. We could ask them if they were itching or if they thought they might have scabies.

Here's what I emailed our Night Coordinators the next day:

"Last night, we conducted a thorough search for unrecognized cases. Kacky spoke with every guest before they entered Calvin Hall through the rear entrance. Of course, they were not happy to enter late (around 8 pm), but they were reassured that if this outbreak (defined as "two or more consecutive cases of scabies within 4-6 weeks") is not gotten under control and treated, I would shut down the shelter."

"Kacky discovered that it is likely that Guest B also has scabies. Last night, we isolated Guests B and C in the space where the cots are stored. They are not to use the cots. Their clothing and blankets have been placed in sealed plastic bags with their names on them. They will be washed using hot water and hot dryer cycles."

"Guest B was given a sleeping bag and mats to use... both which he disinfected this morning and put into black plastic bags and stored separately in the back room. Guest C was given two mats and black plastic bags for his bedding/mats... which he disinfected (the mats) and put into black plastic bags in the back room, as well... in the same place where Guest B's stuff is. Guest A didn't spend the night."

"This morning (Saturday), I paid for a taxi to take Guests A and C to the emergency room to be checked out. Guest D wanted to go to be checked out, as well. Both are supposed to report back before entering the shelter this evening."

What happened next was remarkable! Various members of our community -- volunteers, guests, staff, Health Department -- all stepped up. Joan Kalvelage, a host, emailed more information: "Non-crusting scabies is transmitted only with prolonged body-to-body contact (not just hugs or handshakes) or prolonged exposure to blankets, clothing, etc. Thanks to your initiating the numbering of blankets, contagion is therefore not a big threat. However, several numbered blankets are missing."

"Last night," she wrote, "I brought some tea tree oil (recommended by the CDC for killing scabies mites) to the Presbyterian (church). I would be happy to bring it to other shelters next week ... so hosts have the option of using it to protect themselves and swab scabies sores."

She added, "If any guest with itch problems follows Kristin's request to get diagnosed and treated for the scabies itch, they will then need to wash their clothes. Neither Guests A and C have a change of clothes, so I bought $15 Bi-Mart gift certificates which could be kept in your volunteer binder until (and if) any scabies-infected guest gets a prescription which will render him non-contagious within 2 days, although it may take up to 3 weeks to eliminate the itch. A $15 a gift certificate will buy sweatpants and a shirt on sale so that the guest can wash his or her usual clothes in hot water and dry (on hot setting) for at least 1/2 hour." Thank you, Joan!

I reached out to Dr. Jim Shames with the Oregon Health Department to ask if we needed to report it. "I am not sure you need to report this to anybody," he replied. "But I will pass this on to Public Health. Sounds like you are doing a great job with this."

Dr. Shames and a colleague from La Clinica agreed to come to the shelter. They checked out Guests A, B and C as well as other guests who were concerned about contracting scabies. No cases of scabies were identified.

Some of the guests were still itching and scratching. We created a scabies protocol that three guests decided to follow anyway. It worked, too. The itching symptoms went away.

# Opportunity 9: Team Building

### "Ad Hoc" (Temporary) Teams

I like teams and groups that are "ad hoc," with a clear beginning, middle and end. The team comes together and identifies their primary purpose, timeline and specific outcomes. What happens in the middle is simply the process of completing the tasks according to timeline or outcomes. At the end, we celebrate the completion. Then, we're done!

Our community's mission -- after we discovered that Pioneer Hall would not be available any longer for shelter -- was simple: to find a single location for winter shelter. That's why the name "One Site" was so appropriate.

Some teams can complete their tasks super fast, too.

Take, for example, the Criteria Sub-Committee of the larger One Site Committee. At the April 5, 2018, meeting (our first), we created this team of interested people charged with coming up with a yardstick we could use when checking out buildings being considered. We met right after the One Site meeting.

The meeting took only 30 minutes. We generated a list of "required" and "preferred" criteria for buildings:

Required
- Capacity for 50 guests
- Minimum of 34 square feet per guest = 2,200 square feet
- Sprinklers that meet fire codes
- Minimum of 2 bathrooms

- Meets Americans with Disabilities Act (ADA) of 1990 standards

Preferred

- Place to serve food and clean up (sink, kitchen, refrigerator, etc.)
- Access to showers
- Access to laundry facilities

Poof! It took only 30 minutes! That's all it took to come up with this list. We reported back at the next One Site committee meeting. That's it! We were done! The Criteria Sub-Committee did its job. We never had to meet again!

How great would it feel to have many of our committees and teams finish their jobs early and would not have to meet again!


## Stepping Up

When I was volunteering at the shelter in the first two winter seasons, when Heidi was the coordinator of volunteers, I looked for places where I might make a difference. One example is the online signup form that Heidi had developed. It was a Google Sheet with a link given out for easy access. Volunteers could log in and to put their names and phone numbers for the days that they would like to volunteer for specific jobs.

Jobs included overnight hosts, listeners, food servers, helpers, clean up crews. All jobs and dates were on that spreadsheet. One of the things that I saw right away was that it took a while to scroll through all the dates for 122 nights that were listed chronologically.

I suggested that we create tabs at the bottom for each night we could make it easier for people to navigate. Every day of the week -- Sunday through Saturday -- could have a tab at the bottom. Viewers click on the tab at the bottom and go directly to the page to find the day for which they were looking.

Improving Heidi's spreadsheet was one way of "stepping up."

A second example of "stepping up" happened for me on April 5, 2018, in the lower level of the Ashland Library. At the end of the planning meeting on the future of the winter shelter, I remember thinking that all of this momentum and these great ideas that were generated in this meeting would likely fizzle out unless I literally stepped up, went to the whiteboard and mind-mapped what had just happened in the meeting.

I stood up and walked to the whiteboard. I proceeded to summarize the various ideas that the group had discussed: a governor's possible declaration of a state of emergency, car parking options, city/county planning, other alternatives, funding and sustainability, etc. I grabbed a marker and wrote on the board the names of what would soon become our sub-committees. To each sub-committee, I added names of people who agreed to "chair" each sub-committee or serve as a member:

| Sub-Committee Name | Chair | Members |
| --- | --- | --- |
| Alternatives | Phil | Avram |
| Budget, Fundraising & Sustainability | Peter | Peter, Linda, John, Joan, Mori, Ann, Cathy |
| Car Parking Options | John | John, Linda, Heidi |
| Criteria for 1-Site | Phil | Phil, Kathy, Helga |
| Food & Meals | Vanessa | Cathy |
| Governor Emergency Declaration | Vanessa | Mori, Joan |
| Government Planning | Linda | Linda, Phil, Heidi, Mori, Ron, Tom, Rich |
| Listening | Bob M. | Cathy |

Many individuals and groups stepped up: hundreds of volunteers, 15 night coordinators, 12 community partners and their leadership, local media, and others who haven't been mentioned here.

## Self-Care

Without self-care of volunteers, the winter shelter would have closed down. There's lots to do to set up the space, prepare and serve the food, do the fire watch, spend the night, clean up, and even listening to guests night-after-night.

Common health risks come and go with winter seasons. Freezing temperatures often trigger asthma symptoms. Viruses are passed and picked up more easily in confined spaces with others who may have come down with a cold or flu.

It's important for volunteers to really take care of themselves. It's important for guests to take care of themselves. Self-care is more than a one-person job!

In my case. I was putting in some 20-hour days and some 80 hour-weeks. Fortunately, Kacky Hoffman noticed at one point that I was more stressed than usual, and I might crash. I started having a sore throat. I started coughing.

Kacky made some chicken noodle soup and brought it to me. It hit the spot, too. This came at the perfect time where I was feeling like I was starting to come down with something. It made all the difference.

Likewise, it was wonderful to see how guests and volunteers watch out for each other. When somebody was especially cranky or tired or showing signs of being sick, they'd suggest that we let him take the night off if we could find a replacement.

In one specific case, a few volunteers noticed that one of our amazing hosts was starting to get a little bit run down. Thanks to David Wick (Executive Director) and the Ashland Culture of Peace Commission, we were able to get her a dinner for two at a local restaurant so she could do something nice for herself and her husband. She was so appreciative.

Self-care is an opportunity for full community engagement, too. We look out for each other.

It was amazing to watch guests looking out for each other, too. A newcomer to Ashland helps put on socks and shoes and spends the morning with a developmentally disabled lady. In the *Gloves for Matt* story, Dale gives up his own gloves.

Setting aside one's own personal, in-crisis needs in order to help care for somebody else with even more pressing needs... WOW! That's impressive! It shows such character.

## Finding the Right Fit

Heidi Parker found her role as volunteer coordinator of the winter shelter for six seasons! She saw a volunteer base in Ashland that she could tap into to help our most vulnerable have a roof over their heads in the coldest nights of the year.

Getting funding for a replacement for Heidi as volunteer coordinator and assisting her was a good fit for me. When I decided to apply for Heidi's job, it was also a natural fit for me and my skill set and experience in project management.

Several challenges presented themselves immediately when we started, such as securing additional funding needed for rapid expansion in the 2018-19 season as well as future seasons. Also, a Type II application to Jackson County for a seasonal use permit of the Rogue Valley Church had to be prepared quickly.

In addition, we basically had to open six winter shelters in 2018-19. First, we had seven-nights-per-week shelter in four different locations for 153 nights. Then, when temperatures dropped below 20 degrees, an Extreme Weather Warming Center was opened (a fifth site) for another 11 nights (total = 164 nights). While we waited for Jackson County to approve the permit, we prepared Rogue Valley Church (a sixth site) for occupancy.

Luckily, we had a great team of community partners and volunteers with skills and willingness to make it all work.

There were also many examples of people finding their right fit, too. In the 2017-18 season, Kacky Hoffman applied her interviewing skills to conduct a survey of 57 shelter guests. As she points out in the AHA & WOW Moments chapter, sleeping overnight didn't work for her. Interviewing did!

We had an amazing group of fourteen Night Coordinators: Alex Reid, Bob Morse, Karen Amarotico, Bob Altaras, Avram Sacks, Heidi Parker, Sharon Harris, Kristin Dilling-Conand, Peter McBennett, Mary Bonney, John Wieczorek, Mark Goodman-Morris, Vanessa Houk, Jason Houk. Others who assisted in various capacities were Kacky Hoffman, Joan Kalvelage and Lisa Ostos.

Night Coordinators filled very important roles:

- To identify 2 Night Coordinators to represent Night Sponsor
- To recruit co-hosts to spend the night
- To recruit food preparers, deliverers and servers
  - Dinner (7:30-8:30 pm)
  - Breakfast (6-7 am)
- To welcome listeners
- To coordinate cleanup crew

They mentored hosts-in-training, attended regular Night Coordinator meetings and were encouraged to participate in screening and exiting meetings addressing specific guest cases. They even found their own replacements.

In the Listening Project chapter, Bob Morse shares how listeners found good fits for themselves in ways that benefited hosts and larger numbers of guests. Even groups and organizations found good fits for themselves.

Seven faith-based and nonprofit groups found good fits as Night Sponsors for seven-nights-a-week:

- Sunday: South Mountain Friends Meeting (Quakers)
- Monday: First Presbyterian Church
- Tuesday: Temple Emek Shalom
- Wednesday: Trinity Episcopal
- Thursday: Rogue Valley Unitarian Universalist Fellowship
- Friday: United Congregational Church of Christ
- Saturday: Southern Oregon Jobs With Justice

## Finding the Right Fit for Guests

My vision for One Site (Rogue Valley Church) is that "guests basically run the shelter" as much as possible. We started moving in that direction in the 2018-19 winter shelter season, although it was more challenging doing so at four different venues. This meant that volunteers often arrived to set up at 7 pm and then clean up in the morning and be out by 7 am, so that we could clean the space before the groups renting the space arrived.

On many occasions, guests were involved in the set up and clean up. They swept and mopped the floors and cleaned the women's and men's bathrooms. They picked up cigarette butts and trash around the building, as well as took out the trash.

In this picture, Chris (a guest) is picking up tiles that blew off the roof of the Rogue Valley Church (One Site)! He also helped Peter McBennett with repairs of the building.

Starting in November 2019 at One Site, guests should be able to take on even greater roles. Guests will be able to arrive as early as 6 pm; they won't have to leave until 10 am.

Guests can be trained to run the coat room (to check in personal belongings) and outdoor long-term storage unit. They can assist with set up of tables and chairs for dinner and cots for sleeping. They can vacuum the carpet in the mornings.

Seven nights per week will be at one location, used entirely for the shelter. This will allow for many creative projects that involve guests! I'm excited to see how the guests will be involved in running the shelter moving forward!

## Guests Help with Setup - Thursday Nights

To give you an example of how guests were involved last winter shelter season, let's look at one evening. Every Thursday for twenty-one weeks, the shelter was held at Rogue Valley Unitarian Universalists Fellowship (RVUUF) church on Fourth Street in Ashland. It's a beautiful building and sanctuary. Comfortable, blue chairs are lined up in rows of 8 chairs each.

At 6 pm, two-to-three "paid" guests (who were hired from the Job Target program at the Ashland Community Resource Center) would arrive. We would turn on the lights, wrap caution tape around areas that were blocked off to guests.

We proceeded to unhook each of 200+ chairs and stack them 4 high. There was a special technique, too, to picking up the chairs (so as to not tilt them backwards). Otherwise, the song books on the bottom shelf of the chair fell out on the floor.

We put coasters under the legs of the stacked chairs so they wouldn't dig in the carpet when we slid them across the carpet. We would slide the chairs from one side of the room against the wall. Chairs from the other side of the room would also be lifted and placed into stacks of 4. Coasters were placed under the legs. These were moved to the other side of the Great Hall, next to the wall with the windows.

Once all chairs were stacked and moved to the sides, guests and volunteers went out to the shelter trailer parked outside. We brought in a few dozen bins of mats and blankets to be arranged neatly in the newly opened space based on the layout approved by the Ashland Fire Marshal (created by Ken Gudger... thanks, Ken!).

At 6:30 pm, Mitzie Loftus (or her replacement), a volunteer, would arrive, plug in the coffee and water pots and prepare space in the foyer for the evening meal of leftovers dropped off by volunteers.

It took approximately 75 minutes to set up.

Doors would open at 7:30 pm. Guests would be welcomed and invited in. Many would enter, find a mat and blanket, drop their backpacks and lay down. They were tired and ready to go to sleep. Others would grab some food, coffee or tea. Often they had to be reminded that no food or beverages would be allowed in the Great Hall.

The stain glass mural behind the stage was lit up, too. It was a beautiful backdrop for this make-shift shelter.

Lights went out around 9 pm. Doors were locked at 9:30 pm. If they wanted to leave, they were told, "If you want to go out that's fine. You just can't come back in." Few left.

In the morning, at 6 am, lights turned back on. Coffee would be ready in the lobby, along with food such as breakfast muffins, hard boiled eggs and food items that can be carried, like breakfast bars. Mats would be sanitized, rolled up and placed back in the bins (six per bin). For extra precaution, blankets would be bagged. Guest names were written on the bags. We washed blankets every 4-5 usages.

By 7 am, most were out the door. Of course, there were the usual stragglers who complained about being asked to move faster than they wanted. It's hard to leave a warm place into the freezing cold.

Our guest workers and overnight hosts (volunteers) would take the bins back to the trailer. Floors would be vacuumed, and outside area swept.

Stacks of chairs were slid across the floor and lined back up in rows of eight. There were small pieces of tape placed on the carpet where the legs of the last chairs in each row of eight were to be placed at the inside and outside rows. A long string was used to make sure the inside chairs all lined up.

It took an hour-and-a-half every Friday morning to clean up and put the chairs back! Workers were out by 8:30 am, sometimes earlier if there was another event at the church.

Processes like this were repeated every night for 162 nights at four different churches!

In the case of using Calvin Hall at the First Presbyterian Church of Ashland on Friday, Saturday and Sunday nights, 36 bunk cots (34 for guests and 2 for overnight hosts) had to be unstacked from storage and set out according to a map. Both cots and blankets were numbered. This ensured that people had the same cot and blankets, night after night.

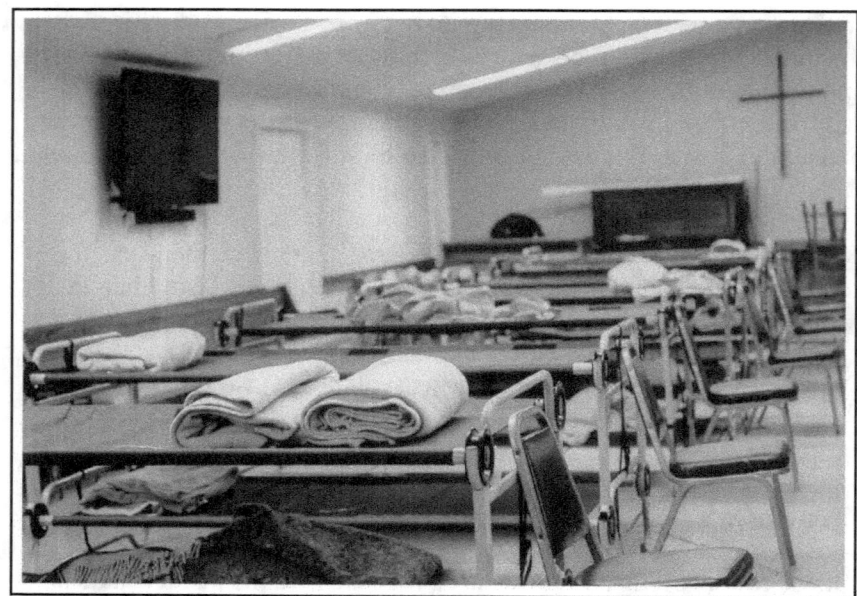

Photo by Jean-Francŏus Durand (www.francous.com)

In the next section (Mindset Shift 3), you will discover the value of community partnerships over working in silos and going it alone

# Mindset Shift 3
# From-Silos-to-Community-Partnerships

*"You never change things by fighting the existing reality. To change something, build a new model that makes the existing model obsolete."* ~Buckminster Fuller

Mindset Shift 3 will empower you and your community to move from doing everything alone or in silos to broaden your community partnerships. A common goal could be to assist your unhoused neighbors along a continuum to become "self-sufficient" and even "thriving" by understanding the "self-sufficiency matrix" and focusing on three important elements of successful collaborations:

1. Create Systems
2. Create Processes
3. Build Partnerships

## Element 1 - Create Systems

### System A - One Site Committee (Community Engagement)

*No More Pioneer Hall*

Built in 1921, Pioneer Hall is a quaint building next to Lithia Park that is owned by the City of Ashland. It had been used as a "drop in" shelter for a number of years. The 2017-18 winter shelter season increased the number of nights of shelter from two to four with a fifth night if temperatures dropped below 20 degrees. However, that was about to change.

In March 2018, we received news that Pioneer Hall would not be available any more for winter shelter unless a new fire sprinkler system, updates to the chimney and other renovations were made that might cost over $350,000 which was unlikely due to budget constraints and established funding priorities.

Right away, meetings were set up to begin exploring what the community might do now with no Pioneer Hall in our future. I was not initially drawn to attending these meetings. We were wrapping up the 2017-18 winter shelter season. I needed a break, having volunteered for 10 consecutive months. However, it was too important to not sit on the sidelines.

**ONE**SITE

ASHLAND'S WINTER SHELTER

First, we needed a name. Since we were all primarily interested in one goal: **find a single site** alternative to Pioneer Hall, I blurted that we should call ours the "One Site Committee." Everyone agreed. The name stuck!

Vanessa Houk collected names, emails and phone numbers from people in attendance. We agreed to meet as a group every three weeks (April 26, June 6, June 27, July 27, August 8, August 28). We agreed that chairpersons would convene sub-committee meetings and report back at One Site committee meetings. Jason Houk made sure we had a room reserved in Ashland Library for our meetings.

### The Power of "One"

*"The illusion is that we are separate."* ~The Course of Miracles

Little did I know at the time that the name "One Site" would serve as such a unifying force that would not only coalesce our committee's energies to find a single location for winter shelter, but would also serve to unify the entire community as well.

Why? "One" is actually a spiritual, unifying principle found in many religious traditions including "yoga" and the lesser known "Advaita" tradition of India.

#### Yoga

According to Wikipedia, "the Sanskrit noun योग *yoga* is derived from the root *yuj* 'to attach, join, harness, yoke.' The word 'yoga' is cognate with English 'yoke'. (It is a) ... philosophical system presented in the Yoga Sutras of Patanjali, with the chief aim of 'uniting' the human spirit with the Divine."

#### Advaita

According to Dr. Gay Hendricks in *Already Home*, "Advaita, a Sanskrit word that means 'not two,' is the name generally given to the long tradition of teachings on nondualism. Although it is most often associated with sages of Hinduism and the Indian subcontinent, nondualism also plays an important role in Zen, mystical Islam, Judaism, and Christianity."

"Nondualism is not a religion in itself, nor is it really a philosophy. It refers to an experience of unity between the experiencer and the object. So, when a practitioner of meditation feels the separation dissolve between herself and God -- when there is no 'I' and God but a unity of the two -- this is exactly what the lineage of Advaita is based on."

Dr. Hendricks adds, "Advaita is about unity, not divisiveness, and there is no question that the times we live in are fraught with division. At a time in history when concepts of God divide so many, the unifying quality of nondualism strikes a harmonious chord in the heart and soul."

The unifying force of "One Site" was emerging in the small town of Ashland!

### *"One" Community: Clergy Letter*

Coincidently, around the same time, a letter supporting the power of "one" from Ashland's Interfaith Clergy Circle appeared in the *Ashland Tidings* (June 2018) signed by over 50 clergy and Ashland residents.

"We believe we are in a time of great opportunity," wrote Ashland's spiritual leaders. "The need for day and night shelter is clear. We ask for the generosity of the comfortable, the stewardship of the professional, the compassion of the faithful, and the leadership of the political."

"We need one place. A sustaining place. A transforming place. A uniting place. In the face of years of effort by churches, leaders, and community members, it is unconscionable to imagine November arriving and there still not being a place for our homeless neighbors."

Thank you, clergy!

## System B - Shelter & Maslow's Hierarchy of Needs

I remember hearing about Abraham Maslow's Hierarchy of Needs in college. I remember that before a person can focus on psychological and self-actualized needs, basic food, clothing and shelter needs must be met. Even though it is technically called a "theory" and not a "system", it is a helpful "model" to understand the system that is required to serve the homeless. The most immediate needs of the homeless fall in the "physiological" needs level of food, clothing and shelter and "safety" needs of security and stability.

By meeting these immediate "basic" needs (along with rest, sleep and warmth) in a winter shelter setting and having a bed for the season (as a result of our new model), our unhoused neighbors are able to achieve and sustain a degree of stability that will allow them to focus their attention on safety needs (security) as well as psychological needs (belonging, love, friendship, accomplishment, etc.) and finally self-sufficient needs (creative expression, achieving one's full potential, etc.).

This was very important to the guests, too. Kacky Hoffman, the end-of-program interviewer, told me, "Going night-to-night not knowing where they would sleep leads to this big insecurity, this horrible existential insecurity. But knowing they had a place every night for the entire shelter season was a big deal that came through loud and clear. Being with the same people, even if they didn't like them, was a significant grounding for them."

## System C - Path to Self-Sufficiency

Most of our homeless guests come to us with no-to-low incomes "in crisis."

As mentioned earlier, in order to achieve self-sufficiency and economic security, we first assess their immediate need for essential services (i.e., health insurance, IDs, phones, SNAP food stamps, etc.) and then assess more long-term needs by employing a self-sufficiency matrix.

**The result is an individualized roadmap from "crisis" of immediate need to temporary support stability on a path to "self-sufficiency" and even "thriving".**

### *Background - Self-Sufficiency Matrix*

According to PerformWell, a collaborative effort initiated by Urban Institute, Child Trends, and Social Solutions, "the self-sufficiency matrix is an assessment and outcome measurement tool based on the federal outcomes standard ROMA (Results Oriented Management and Accountability). This impact measurement tool has 25 individual scales, each measuring observable change in some aspect of self-sufficiency."

Each scale can be measured using five levels:

Level 1 - Crisis
Level 2 - Vulnerable
Level 3 - Stable (or Safe)
Level 4 - Self-Sufficient
Level 5 - Empowered (or Thriving)

"The matrix is designed to be flexible: any combination of scales can be used, based on the goals and strategies of individual programs. In addition, each scale was developed independently on a continuum from 'in-crisis' to 'thriving' and allows for the measurement of client progress or maintenance over time."

For example, let's take a look to see how the self-sufficiency matrix can be used in three important categories: employment, housing and legal.

*Self-Sufficiency Matrix Scale: EMPLOYMENT*

What does this scale measure? The employment scale assesses the nature of the job or career in which the client is employed and considers the permanency and stability of the job, as well as the benefits that accompany employment:

Level 1 - No job.
Level 2 - Temporary, part-time or seasonal; inadequate pay, no benefits.
Level 3 - Employed full time; inadequate pay; few or no benefits.
Level 4 - Employed full time with adequate pay and benefits.
Level 5 - Maintains permanent employment with adequate income and benefits.

*Self-Sufficiency Matrix Scale: HOUSING*

The housing scale assesses the household's current housing situation:

Level 1 - Homeless or threatened with eviction.
Level 2 - In transitional, temporary or substandard housing; and/or current rent/mortgage payment is unaffordable (over 30% of income).
Level 3 - In stable housing that is safe but only marginally adequate.
Level 4 - Household is in safe, adequate subsidized housing.
Level 5 - Household is safe, adequate, unsubsidized housing.

*Self-Sufficiency Matrix Scale: LEGAL – CRIMINAL JUSTICE*

The legal scale assesses both past and present involvement with law enforcement and other elements of the criminal justice system:

Level 1 - Current outstanding tickets or warrants.
Level 2 - Current charges/trial pending, noncompliance with probation/parole.
Level 3 - Fully compliant with probation/parole terms.
Level 4 - Has successfully completed probation/parole within the past 12 months, no new charges filed.
Level 5 - No active criminal justice involvement in 12 months and/or no felony criminal history.

According to the The Snohomish County Self-Sufficiency Taskforce, the Self-Sufficiency Matrix has many applications for programs interested in solutions for ending homelessness:

1. "As a CASE MANAGEMENT TOOL for case workers as they work with individual clients and document progress towards self-sufficiency over time at specific intervention points or, when appropriate, to document a client's ability to maintain a certain level of functioning. The Matrix is an effective and efficient tool for documenting the progress or maintenance of client skills and abilities by providing a clear illustration of where a client has strengths, as well as where to focus additional energy to generate improvement.

2. As a SELF-ASSESSMENT TOOL for individuals who wish to determine their own strengths and areas for improvement as they work towards self-sufficiency. This application of the tool is similar to its use as a case management tool.

3. As a MANAGEMENT TOOL for programs and agencies to determine what is and isn't working in terms of the type of services offered to clients and the way those services are delivered. The Matrix allows program staff to identify where additional resources are needed and how to deploy those resources most effectively.

4.  As a MEASUREMENT TOOL, both for funders and
    organizations that receive grant funding. The Matrix provides
    funders a way to clearly articulate their funding priorities to
    interested applicants and to the community at-large by using
    specific scales on the matrix to articulate funding priorities or
    primary interests. For programs that are widely using this tool,
    the Self-Sufficiency Matrix can serve as a way to consolidate
    outcomes for multiple clients and report results to funders.
5.  As a COMMUNICATION TOOL for demonstrating the success
    of local programs, as well as sharing information about
    community conditions with both the general public and
    policymakers. As use of the Matrix continues to grow, it
    promises to be an effective communication tool for illustrating
    the strengths, as well as weaknesses, of our community to help
    families work towards self-sufficient living. In addition, a
    collective analysis of the results generated by programs using the
    Self-Sufficiency Matrix will aid the community and policy
    makers in their understanding of what self-sufficiency looks like
    in Snohomish County, what barriers exist for families working
    towards self-sufficiency, and where system-level efforts are
    required to improve opportunities for low-income working
    families."

# Element 2 - Create Processes

## Process A - Screening & Selecting Guests

Ashland's Winter Shelter welcomes all people who are homeless unless they have previously been banned due to severe violence towards staff or another guest or dealing drugs on our property. Those individuals with high contagious, communicable diseases may be restricted (from infecting other shelter guests) until appropriately treated and deemed safe.

Screening takes place off-site at the Ashland Community Resource Center (ACRC) next to Safeway in Ashland. Trained interviewers use the Vulnerability Index - Service Prioritization Decision Assistance Tool (VI-SPDAT). Results from the screening were entered into the Homelessness Management Information System (HMIS).

Selection (deciding who to let into the shelter) involves VI-SPDAT information as well as the judgment of community partners, ACRC staff and volunteers who are often familiar with applicants. When there were open beds, meetings were called. Night Coordinators and staff were invited everyone to discuss all applicants and make recommendations for selection.

## Process B - Welcoming Guests

### First Night

On the first night of Ashland's Winter Shelter, we welcomed our guests who did not participate in the Orientation. We interviewed each guest with a Welcoming Form like this:

| ESSENTIAL SERVICE | CURRENTLY HAS? | WOULD LIKE? |
|---|---|---|
| **Oregon Health Plan (OHP)** __Jackson Care Connect __Allcare __Private | | |
| **Identification (ID)** __Birth Certificate __Driver's License __SS Card __ID | | |
| **Phone #**_____ __Assurance Wireless/Lifeline (Free) | | |
| **Bus Pass** Type_____ | | |
| **SNAP/Food Stamps** | | |
| **Mailbox** | | |

Our goal was that within 1 week, 100% of our shelter guests would have all of these essential services in place. 1-week results "inspired" guests to begin to move along the continuum of care from "crisis" to "self-sufficiency" in multiple categories that would then become the focus of year-round case management and support: housing, employment, education, recovery from substance abuse, money management, mental health, legal assistance, support systems, etc.

Shelter guests frequently report back beaming with pride: "I'm using my bus passes to get dental work done and go to work." "I'm 1-month drug-free." "I'm 5 weeks sober." "I just got accepted into Rogue Community College."

Previously, the Self-Sufficiency Matrix was explained in detail. During the first night of shelter, we asked guests if they had (or would like) six essential services included two categories of self-sufficiency: transportation and health care access. By providing transportation (bus passes) and ensuring everyone has full-coverage healthcare (Oregon

Health Plan, Veteran Administration, or other), we eliminated two substantial barriers to seeking medical care (physical and/or mental)!

## *Transportation*

Guests immediately move from "in-crisis" to "stable" along the self-sufficiency matrix in the category of "transportation". Most of their transportation needs are met through public transportation. 3,792 bus rides were purchased. Shelter guests use their passes (6 rides) to get to places where they can work on their housing plans, secure benefits, search for jobs, make and keep appointments, seek healthcare, look for housing, go to work, access showers and meals, go to AA meetings, counseling, and more.

*Self-Sufficiency Scale: TRANSPORTATION*

The transportation scale assesses whether or not the individual has appropriate, safe and reliable access to transportation (whether by car, bus or reliance on friends/family):

Level 1 - No access to transportation, public or private; may have car that is inoperable.
Level 2 - Transportation is available, but unreliable, unpredictable, unaffordable; may have care but no insurance, license, etc.
Level 3 - Transportation is available and reliable, but limited and/or inconvenient; drivers are licensed and minimally insured.
Level 4 - Transportation is generally accessible to meet basic travel needs.
Level 5 - Transportation is readily available and affordable; car is adequately insured.

As a result of having bus passes, guests progressed quickly from level 1 (crisis) to level 4 (self-sufficient).

*Health Care*

100% of our guests had full health care coverage. Guests were able to seek more regular and preventive care and to access mental health services. They have reduced financial anxiety and burden of seeking care. By ensuring our guests have medical coverage, they were able to seek primary preventative care and/or timely care for medical issues. It reduced the need for ambulance and emergency trips.

It protected the entire shelter population from outbreaks common in shelter settings such as scabies and pneumonia.

*Self-Sufficiency Scale: HEALTH CARE ACCESS*

The health care scale assesses need for health care, as well as access to both health care and medical insurance coverage:

Level 1 - No medical coverage with immediate need.
Level 2 - No medical coverage and great difficulty accessing medical care when needed. Some household members may be in poor health.
Level 3 - Some members (like Children) have medical coverage.
Level 4 - All members can get medical care when needed, but may strain budget.
Level 5 - All members are covered by affordable, adequate health insurance.

As a result of full medical coverage, guests progressed quickly from level 1 (crisis) to level 4 (self-sufficient).


## Process C - Exiting Guests

Exiting guests from the shelter -- asking them to leave temporarily or permanently -- is something that I had mixed feelings about in past seasons. Why? Because there was no consistency in making the call.

The process used by various overnight hosts to exit people was different in the past. Often "exiting" required calling the police.

## *Results: Reduced Police Calls by 92%*

In 82 nights at Pioneer Hall in 2017-18, there were 24 calls to Ashland Police Department. This means that there was one call for every four nights of shelter.

The large number was largely the result of the chaotic nature of the "drop in" system. Everyone was allowed in on a "first come, first served" basis. It was a powder-keg-ready-to-explode. It did, too.

What difference did the new "pre-screened" model make?

In the first 82 nights in the 2018-19 winter shelter season, there were only 2 police calls. That's a 92% reduction in the number of police calls. That's one call for every 41 nights!

Even without calling the police for help, exiting guests for breaking community rules (see Guest Agreement Form in Appendix C) is absolutely necessary. If there was a physical altercation, someone was exited.

To assist with the process, we implemented an Incident Report form (see Appendix D), which was filled out after an event. Sometimes "exiting" was recommended by the host on duty. Usually, it was not.

I reviewed all incident reports. I spoke with all parties involved. When the decision was not clear cut, I often sought advice from multiple people on our team.

All exiting decisions were aligned with the breaking of a specific community rule that appears in the Guest Agreement Form.


## Process D - Re-Entry Plans

Re-Entry Plans are customized or tailor-made for individuals who are "exited" for bad behavior such as bullying. An incident report would have been filed. Conversations would have taken place with affected parties.

During the "exiting" interview with the guest, we would sit down with them in private, outside of the shelter at a different location. We would discuss what it would take for them to re-enter the shelter, if they so desired.

Re-Entry Plans would be agreed upon, written down and signed (and dated) by guests. Written plans would include specific actions to be taken to ensure everyone's safety and rectify any broken agreements. It may include apologizing to another person (guest or host) or enrolling in a 12-step, mental health or anger management program to develop specific skills.

Re-Entry Plans were "redemptive". They give people a second chance. Of course, if we exited guests for breaking some "soft" rules, such as being respectful of others, we wouldn't have anybody left in the shelter. As long as there is a fair and safe process in place that honors the rights of everyone in the shelter, Re-Entry Plans can result in helping people to master life skills and community skills they need to live and "thrive" in a group living situation.

# Element 3 - Build Partnerships

## 12 Community Partners

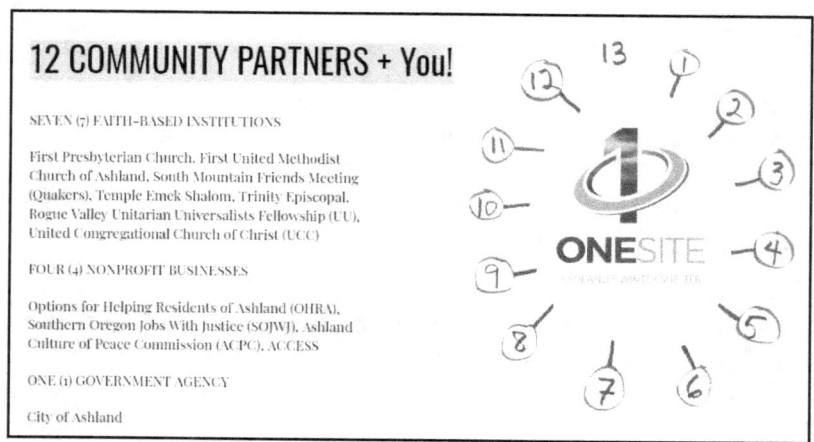

**12 COMMUNITY PARTNERS + You!**

SEVEN (7) FAITH-BASED INSTITUTIONS

First Presbyterian Church, First United Methodist Church of Ashland, South Mountain Friends Meeting (Quakers), Temple Emek Shalom, Trinity Episcopal, Rogue Valley Unitarian Universalists Fellowship (UU), United Congregational Church of Christ (UCC)

FOUR (4) NONPROFIT BUSINESSES

Options for Helping Residents of Ashland (OHRA), Southern Oregon Jobs With Justice (SOJWJ), Ashland Culture of Peace Commission (ACPC), ACCESS

ONE (1) GOVERNMENT AGENCY

City of Ashland

ONESITE

Our 12 community partners consisted of seven (7) faith-based institutions:

- First Presbyterian Church (night sponsor) (venue)
- First United Methodist Church of Ashland (venue)
- South Mountain Friends Meeting (Quakers) (night sponsor)
- Temple Emek Shalom (night sponsor)
- Trinity Episcopal (night sponsor) (venue)
- Rogue Valley Unitarian Universalists Fellowship (UU) (night sponsor) (venue)
- United Congregational Church of Christ (UCC)] (night sponsor)

...four (4) Nonprofit Organizations:

- Options for Helping Residents of Ashland (OHRA)
- Southern Oregon Jobs With Justice (SOJWJ) (night sponsor)
- Ashland Culture of Peace Commission (ACPC)
- Aging Community Coordinated Enterprises & Supportive Services, Inc. (ACCESS)

... one (1) local government agency: the City of Ashland.

Seven Night Sponsors (listed above) committed to:

- Identify 2 Night Coordinators to represent Night Sponsor
- Recruit co-hosts to spend the night (7:30 pm - 7:30 am)
- Recruit food preparers, deliverers and servers for dinner (7:30-8:30 pm) and breakfast (6-7 am)
- Sign in/out volunteers in the evening and morning
- Coordinate cleanup crew (7-8 am)

Options for Helping Residents of Ashland (OHRA) agreed to:

- Serve as fiscal agent for donations and ACCESS grant funding "flow through"
- Serve as lessor of One Site at 2082 East Main St.
- Submit the Type 2 application to Jackson County for seasonal land use permit for One Site at 2082 East Main St
- Conduct screening of prospective shelter guests at the Ashland Community Resource Center (ACRC)
- Provide related services at ACRC (i.e., housing, employment, mental health, etc.)

- Work to ensure primary transportation for guests coming to/from One Site at a set schedule
- Hire Shelter Consultant (Phil Johncock) to:
  - Develop necessary policies, procedures and behavior standards
  - Coordinate process for "screening" guests
  - Manage record-keeping of guests and volunteers
  - Identify and support Night Sponsors
  - Moderate communication systems between Night Sponsors and Night Coordinators (i.e., monthly meetings, emails, texts, etc.)
  - Maintain an up-to-date roster of screened guests and trained volunteers (including background checks for co-hosts who spend the night)
  - Automate systems for data collection and community rule/policy monitoring
  - Provide updates and summary reports to OHRA
  - Help design and manage emergency shelter process

Ashland Culture of Peace Commission (ACPC) received a grant from the Carpenter Foundation to:

- Assist with recruitment and training of winter shelter volunteers
- Serve as liaison with the Ashland business community

ACCESS is the Community Action Agency for Jackson County. As such, ACCESS receives State Homeless Assistance Program (SHAP) state funding from Oregon Housing and Community Services (OHCS) to "help meet the emergency needs of homeless Oregonians by providing operational support for emergency shelters and supportive services to shelter residents."

The City of Ashland and City Council:

- Helped negotiate with ACCESS for additional SHAP state funding;
- Made an introduction to the Oregon Community Foundation which resulted in funding for internal sprinklers;
- Negotiated an Extreme Weather Warming Center (Warming Center) agreement with OHRA to be offered when temperatures dropped below 20 degrees (11 Warming Centers were offered in 2018-19);

- Coordinated with Ashland Fire Department to help ensure that venues met fire codes;
- Assisted with the creation and revision of the Type 2 Application to Jackson County for a seasonal use permit for One Site at 2082 East Main Street; and
- Supported the use of Pioneer Hall for community meals on Mondays, Wednesdays, Thursdays, Fridays and Saturdays.

In all of my public presentations, I would start by honoring the 12 community partners. Then, I would say, "We're always looking for our 13th community partner. Perhaps that partner could be 'you'."

# Listening Project

One of the unique features of Ashland's Winter Shelter is its Listening Project. Bob Morse, Manager of the Listening Project, describes it this way:

Our unhoused neighbors live at the intersection of invisibility & exposure. The homeless are always in the public eye, but seldom do housed people look street people in the eye. To not feel seen is to feel insignificant and to be marginalized—and to experience being inaudible.

Everyone carries stories in their heart; many people carry stories that are laced with loneliness and fear, especially when living on the street, but also stories of love and caring, and most of these stories go untold.

Anyone with an open heart, an open mind, and a calling to recognize our common humanity is most welcome to provide shelter listening at the winter homeless shelter in Ashland, Oregon.
Many of the shelter guests have experienced trauma. The uncertainty and lack of safety that accompanies life on the streets is traumatizing in and of itself.

Overnight shelter hosts say that when *listening* takes place in the evening, there's less *restlessness* during the night.

The winter homeless shelter in Ashland opens each evening at 7:30 pm. Quiet time takes place starting at 9 pm, and the doors are locked and lights turned out at 9:30 pm. Shelter listening takes place within the initial 90 minutes (7:30 to 9 pm).

When guests first enter, there's a burst of energy until folks settle themselves and their belongings. Then most guests come over to tables to eat a light meal. Sitting with guests while they eat has proven to be a cordial and respectful way to begin to know them.

No specific training is required. For those who wish, there's a monthly Compassionate Listening practice group in Ashland in which they can participate. Most listeners, however, start out by "shadowing" an experienced listener, mostly to get introduced to guests. Conversations tend to be easier to initiate when people know something about each other, even just a first name.

When I say listening, I'm not referring to therapy. We're not necessarily solving problems. We're simply lending a kind ear, a kind eye, and a kind heart. We're listening.

**How did the Listening Project get started?** Here is part of a conversation with Bob Morse:

I was writing articles for the *Ashland Tidings* column. The Culture of Peace Commission has a column in the *Tidings* every two weeks. I was writing articles in a similar process to this. It was a conversation interview.

I gathered about half dozen people from one of many different segments of the community. There were people working on sanctuary, teenagers, artists, activists, people who have lived here a long time.

One time I was interviewing the people who run the shelter, the shelter coordinators, who have been around for a long time. This was probably about nine years ago now. We had maybe a dozen guests per night. We had a chance to sit and talk to them, get to know them. They got to know us.

Then, we started having five dozen people show up a night. We didn't have time to have a conversation with them. Yet, they had important stories to tell.

What came up in the interview for me was a need for listeners. Around that time, the person that wrote the book on Compassionate Listening, Carol Hwoschinsky, lived in Ashland. (Carol's book is entitled *Listening with the Heart - A Guide For Compassionate Listening*.) She was available to do a training on Compassionate Listening. We trained probably a dozen and a half people. We all began listening. The problem was that it was March. The shelter here ended in April. We just kind of got our feet wet, got involved. Then, the season ended.

The next winter shelter season (2017) started with a training for volunteers. The group running the shelter asked me to come up and speak about shelter listening. There was a lot of interest. That's what kindled it for good. At this moment, it has been two-to-three seasons that we've offered listening.

Source: Bob Morse

# AHA & WOW Moments

*"We think sometimes that poverty is only being hungry, naked and homeless. The poverty of being unwanted, unloved and uncared for is the greatest poverty. We must start in our own homes to remedy this kind of poverty."* ~Mother Teresa

In the last 12 months, there have been many magical AHA and WOW moments. AHA moments are those when a light bulb goes off inside. You have an insight.

For example, when we were working on the flyer for the Orientation for Volunteers, we interviewed several graphic artists. Each wanted $250-$500 to design it, and it would take 2-3 weeks. A light bulb went off. "I know a way to get it done cheaper and quicker."

How? I visited the website: *GrafficRiver.net.* I bought a flyer template I liked, then hired the designer who created the template to customize the template for our event. Total cost was $55. Total time from start-to-finish was 3 days. Plus, we could use the template for future volunteer recruitment after the Orientation. See flyer on this page.

That was an AHA moment for me.

WOW moments are those "big energy" moments that make a big impression and often serve as a "call to action" for an individual or group. For example, one WOW moment happened on October 29, 2018, at 2 pm when a small group of us discovered that The Grove building (located at 1195 E Main Street in Ashland) would not be available for shelter for four nights a week. Three hours later, I shared this information with a group of Night Coordinators. I choked up. It was 12 days before the opening of the winter shelter. The last hope for seven-nights-a-week of shelter had disappeared. There was nothing we could do.

While we were emotionally devastated, that desperation created this vacuum. Resources from the community rushed in to fill that emptiness from a sense of urgency. It was miraculous.

For example, one week later, Eileen Picker, Warden for Trinity Episcopal, announced at a City Council Study Session that her church would be willing to offer two nights of shelter. Leadership from two other churches -- First United Methodist Church of Ashland and Rogue Valley Unitarian Universalists Fellowship -- soon followed suit. They stepped up to offer their venues for the remaining two nights.

Very quickly, City Administrator (Kelly Madding) and Ashland Fire Marshal (Ralph Sartain) and church leadership carved out time out of their busy schedules to help us get the two new sites up to fire code for temporary shelter occupancy in less than a week!

Five days later, we opened our doors seven (7) nights a week at four different church venues. WOW, now that was amazing!

Even Ashland's Mayor, John Stromberg, was impressed. In his State of the City address on January 31, 2019, he said, "It exemplifies 'spontaneous collaboration' in a particularly significant way. As the deadline for shelter to open came closer, multiple parties came together and committed resources, facilities, volunteers, money and organizational identity. The Winter Shelter came into existence."

"The City Administrator and City Councillors were involved in significant ways. Nobody got together and said, 'Okay, now we're going to work on this. You work on that. Is this okay if we get this approved?'"

"They just all did it. Now, we have seven nights a week shelter for people. It takes place in a couple of churches. We're hoping to move it to another location relatively soon where it can be seven nights a week in the same place."

# Conversation With Kacky Hoffman

To illustrate the wide range of AHA and WOW moments at Ashland's Winter Shelter, I asked Kacky Hoffman, a volunteer, about her AHA and WOW moments. Here are some excerpts from our conversation:

**Phil:** One AHA moment came with the Interfaith Clergy letter. The timing was uncanny, being published within weeks of naming the One Site. Everything was like coming from a community mind or consciousness. Reverend Richenda Fairhurst with Ashland First United Methodist Church was a key community leader to pull that together and garner support.

Then, the multi-faith Conference that the Interfaith Social Justice Coalition decided to put on on the topic of homelessness on August 8, 2018. I think that was a community WOW moment.

**Kacky:** Yes, that was a strong moment. It just happened on its own. It was true synchronicity. I wish moments like those could be recreated but when they happen. It can be very powerful for a community and for an organization. That's the energy needed when various groups come together with the same vision. It's amazing!

**Phil:** Well, that was really your doing. When you interviewed 57 shelter guests back in December 2017 and January 2018, the Interfaith Social Justice Coalition wanted to hear about the survey results. I took the important data you collected and then shared it with the City Council and then with the Coalition. The survey results were like an invitation to get involved. It challenged people: "Okay, we need to do more" and "Now that we know something about our folks, what can we do?"

**Kacky:** Yes, I forgot about that! I think the data we gathered from the initial survey was so useful because you had no expectations. The questions were designed to paint a clear picture of who was using shelter services in the Ashland community. The interviews I had with shelter guests were just an honest authentic asking. "Let's see who our neighbors are." "Let's see who it is we are serving and trying to support."

After I introduced myself, I presented the survey to each shelter guest in the most private space we could find, given the confines of our busy winter shelter. I explained it was completely optional and that we wanted to gather information on all of our shelter guests in order to determine the needs of the people using shelter services in Ashland.

Up until this time, the Ashland community had provided shelter services, but there was no data collected on where shelter guests were from, how long they had needed shelter in terms of months or years, how old they were, if they had disabilities, etc. The questions asked were respectful of individual needs, and asked in a friendly and conversational way. Some people shared quite a bit about their lives and situations, and some were more private.

We came away with life stories as well hard data and factual information which were critically important to help our community understand who we were serving, and how to build a shelter program around real people with real needs. We found that the people we were serving literally were our neighbors.

I think the survey information changed the thinking in our community from, "It's just a bunch of crazy kids from California that we're feeding and giving shelter" to "No, that's not right, these are our neighbors! These are people have been in Ashland and Jackson County for a long time." And our shelter guests became human beings for the very first time in Ashland.

A survey like this could easily be recreated in other communities with other organizations. It's the first step toward building a shelter program. You need to get to know your population and understand their needs at a human level and find out who they are. After having conversations, gathering the information and data, letting the natural, compassionate part of ourselves and our communities respond. Just naturally respond after absorbing the information

Yes, conducting the survey was absolutely necessary, Phil! I think that worked out well as part of your plan.

**Phil:** While I'm flattered, in reality, none of this was planned. It was all made up in. Your interviews of 57 shelter guests was actually inspired by our guests: Dale. It shed light on the specific needs of our unhoused neighbors. As you say, it was data that humanized homelessness,

90

especially the Interfaith Social Justice group, I think the interview results given on June 11, 2018, touched an "emotional" part of their brains and hearts. They responded with "Yes, and what can we do to help?" Answer: "Well, let's organize a Faith Summit on the problem" which happened August 15, 2018.

On June 4, 2018, when Heidi asked me to share the survey results with the City Council, they decided to create the Group of 5 to look at buildings and properties in Ashland that might be used for shelter.

**Kacky:** Yes, which shows you have to have both data AND emotional context, a humanistic perspective to inspire people to move. You need both. One without the other isn't enough. It worked because we had both.

We collected the real stories of real people and real numbers of those we served at our Ashland shelter. And they were primarily our neighbors. The data we gathered was different from the Point in Time Count (PIT) which is done annually throughout the United States. The PIT is pure data, without stories and names, but it's not personal to our Ashland community and it's not conclusive.

Our survey data was local, and a local person was presenting the information to the community, not someone from the state or the federal government. It was important that person was you, Phil, because people knew you, and saw your integrity because they saw you working the problem every night in the shelter.

That was a strong position for you to be in because you were able to be working on the street as effectively as presenting to different community groups.

**Phil:** Yes. Another group to whom I presented your data was the Board of Directors of First Presbyterian Church of Ashland on June 24, 2018. I was asking for the use of Calvin Hall as the single site location for seven nights a week. I created a list of Frequently Asked Questions (FAQs) which included your interview data (see Appendix A).

I put together the FAQs because I knew that to get people (from the board) on board quickly, I wanted to spend time in the meeting address their unique questions and concerns and refer them to the FAQs if they wanted more information. I wanted to show that I was prepared.

The FAQs gave me confidence going into the meeting. The name One Site and the logo gave us credibility although we were not official. We were a group of social activists and people, lots of people, lots of people in the community, in search of a single location.

**Kacky:** We didn't have major grant money yet either, did we?

**Phil:** No. There was a commitment of $25,000 that Heidi Parker had brought in to hire someone to replace her. There wasn't anything else. Yes, we had zero money. We did have credibility and confidence of previous seasons run by volunteers and Heidi's organization of the Night Coordinators who met monthly during the winter shelter season. In fact, it was at one of the monthly meetings when I first heard that Pioneer Hall would not be available any more. That's another WOW moment.

**Kacky:** Yes, that was a big WOW moment.

**Phil:** Personally, it affected me for at least a month. I couldn't envision the winter shelter continuing with only two nights of shelter. I wasn't excited about going to planning meetings. I was too bummed out. Somehow, probably through Heidi's encouragement, I attended the April 6, 2018, planning meeting. The rest is history.

**Kacky:** Another one for me was in February 2019. I went to the Rotary Club of Ashland lunch where the mayor spoke on the State of the City. As I remember, the majority of his speech was what the Ashland Winter Shelter represented in the community of Ashland. He used it as an example of how beautifully the people of Ashland could work together and what amazing things they could accomplish, if they wanted to.

The mayor's comments made me think more broadly, that the shelter project had a significant impact on our city and perhaps inspired the mayor and other volunteers and community members as well. It illustrates how one little project can actually affect a broader venue than what might have been initially envisioned.

**Phil:** Yes, I didn't see the Rotary presentation but I found another State of the City address the mayor gave at the end of January 2019. He talked about the shelter as a model of community partnership. I think in some way, it was all so surprising to the mayor, out of the blue.

I don't know what made people want to be part of it. Heidi of course did a great job in creating the model with volunteers and Night Sponsors. I've never been part of such an inspiring and successful community partnership. It felt like everyone and every agency really showed up and contributed. Volunteers, community partners, everybody knew their roles.

**Kacky:** Yes, Heidi and all of the volunteers, Night Coordinators and Hosts, had worked for years before you or I became involved in the shelter. They were, and are, amazing. They felt ownership because they started the program and it was their dream. As they contributed, they felt ownership. That was the strength of it. Everyone felt connected, very loyal to the program because they were doing something really worthwhile. Ownership is the key and I hope that spirit continues.

**Phil:** Drill down a little bit deeper into "ownership". Not everybody feels ownership in projects and in things that they're doing.

**Kacky:** I agree. I think many times people are committed to a project, their work or volunteer work because they agreed to do the work but there's not a personal connection. Ownership implies a sense of control and of individual authority. For me, it appeared that the volunteers felt that sense of control because they were so valued.

Volunteering at the shelter can be difficult, emotional work. It calls on us to be present with our whole selves, because after a day on the streets throughout the winter, our shelter guests are often battling not only sometimes extreme weather conditions but, exhaustion, hunger, mental illness, all forms of trauma, abuse issues, physical illness and confusion. It requires a big heart, sense of humor and emotional energy to be present for our guests, and for each other.

Guests and volunteers can often feel insulted or emotionally hurt which requires moments where emotional support needs to be provided to someone who's upset or crying, angry, or who needs understanding and simply needs to be left alone with compassion and monitoring.

It's personal work that requires empathy and compassion every moment. Perhaps ownership comes because it's so deeply personal and emotional for most of the volunteers as well as deeply gratifying. Relationships between guests and volunteers are formed that are built on trust, and are many times the basis for positive changes and growth in the guest's lives.

Whatever the situation, volunteering in the shelter requires a lot from volunteers, on a human level, which is unique in our world. I think sometimes in our communities, we isolate ourselves in our own comfort zones, and we stop connecting on an emotional human level. When you volunteer to work with shelter guests, that comfort zone is gone and you open yourself up to all kinds of emotional triggers.

It's important to keep yourself "in check" to be kind and compassionate no matter what comes at you, because you are the trusted and needed volunteer. At the same time, you may have different values that are in contradiction to the person you are to be helping. You will witness great sadness and suffering in any given moment during the hours of your work. Then, you leave it to return to a safe comfortable life while holding that within yourself. It's all a challenging and deeply personal balance to maintain.

I think the ownership piece is also a precious aspect of this work in the Ashland shelter because of that balance and of continually being faced with the questions, "Why am I so lucky? Why do I have a comfortable, safe life that could so easily, by a twist of fate, have turned out differently? A moment ago, I was with people experiencing more suffering and loss that I will ever know, and now they are still there, and I am comfortable."

The experience of volunteering in this way deepens our humanity and is unique to this work. The fields of medicine, mental health and education, require skills to keep "compassion in check." The same skills are needed when volunteering to work in a shelter.

**Phil:** That's good. When you've got a situation with people with severe crisis and severe problems on so many levels, compassion gets ignited. You may also be triggered by something that's running up against your belief system. "Why should we let people with addiction into the shelter to begin with?" Then, you tap the compassion that this person needs to eat and needs a place to sleep.

You're constantly dancing between the compassion and the challenging of your belief system. It's a paradox: "How can I be in this situation with so much hurt?" People deepen their own experiences too to live with that paradox. They don't run from it, which is remarkable. We didn't have many people who were challenged who walked (or ran) away.

**Kacky:** No, we didn't. Most people continued to volunteer throughout the shelter season, and I believe that's because they felt their work was deeply valued by the guests and by all of the other hundreds of shelter volunteers.

**Phil:** I'd like to ask you about "finding your right fit." When you started, you tried some things that weren't a good fit.

**Kacky:** I came into the shelter as a potential volunteer to observe one night, and I thought being a night host was the only volunteer option. A night host was someone who sleeps overnight at the shelter to ensure guest safety. I knew immediately that I wouldn't be able to fit into that volunteer position and sleep overnight. I am a very light sleeper and being awake for 28-29 hours was not something I could do. I also knew I could be supportive for four to five hours in order to meet guests needs, and deal effectively with any crisis if it should appear, but not for the ten or twelve hours required of a host. However, I did want to help in some capacity.

**Phil:** What shifted? You ended up having that sort of amount of time in meetings? I have a story that it wasn't a good fit for you until you did the survey and interviewed 57 guests. You had the skill set. It was something that you did well.

**Kacky:** As I remember, you talked to me about the survey the first night I observed in the shelter. I am a retired School Psychologist and ran programs, created surveys, and managed and analyzed data in my previous work, so conducting a survey and gathering data on our unhoused Ashland population was a natural place for me to volunteer. My previous work experience showed me how valuable data collection can be when designing a program, and it also made asking questions and gathering life stories natural and enjoyable.

After completing that survey, I learned that shelter guests really wanted a place and time to talk with volunteers and one another so I started a "conversation circle". We met after the dinner on Friday nights at Pioneer Hall. I partnered with Bob Morse from the Listening Project. I continued volunteering as a "listener" and provided meals on Friday nights throughout the past winter.

I found volunteering on committees satisfying, and completed a Transportation Survey for the new shelter building, chaired the Screening

95

and Data Entry/Exit Committee, and helped mentor new staff and mediated conflicts between shelter guests as needed. It turned out that there were indeed many ways for me to be involved as a volunteer.

**Phil:** You also did a survey this winter shelter season (2018-19).

**Kacky:** Yes. I did an end-of-year survey in order to gather impressions from guests on the first year of the new shelter model.

**Phil:** How did that go?

**Kacky:** I think it was very useful and could be used to help shape the shelter program for 2019 – 2020. I asked three simple questions:

1. What was the best thing about being at Ashland's Winter Shelter this year?
2. What was the hardest thing about being in shelter this year?
3. What is something you would change? Then I ask for any good ideas they might have.

The responses were very insightful, and there were some humorous responses to "What was the hardest thing about being in shelter this year?" I found one humorous response from a significant number of the men who said that the "women were fighting with one another too much".

Many guests said that seeing many of the same people every night for all five months of shelter made the shelter "feel like a family". I believe it was because they socialized with the same people. I sensed "family" was something most guests hadn't experienced in a long time because relationships on the street are very fluid and singular.

Living without the security of knowing where they would sleep every night leads to an overwhelming sense of insecurity, a horrible existential insecurity. But knowing they had a place every night for the entire shelter season provided a sense of safety and security for everyone that was interviewed. And being with the same people, even if they didn't like one another, was a significantly grounding and healing.

One of the things guests loved best was sleeping on cots instead of on the floor. They loved the cots at Presbyterian Church. They also loved the food that we provided at the shelter, and said when they came into the shelter in the evening and had a warm place with food; it made them feel "homey and good".

Regarding what they would like to change, guests stated they wanted to have the same rules in every shelter site, on every night. I felt perhaps they wanted that consistency because of the inconsistent, chaotic life they live on the street during the day. The guest appreciated the rules and wished they were enforced more clearly and at every single site. That surprised me a bit because I thought they might prefer to just come and go as they please. That wasn't the case. I feel the rules were felt to keep them safe, and keep things equitable.

**Phil:** Did they say why that was important for them?

**Kacky:** The guests reported that enforcing shelter rules with consistency and showing respect were important to them. It was important that volunteers treated them with respect, and ensured they treat each other with respect. Also, they found it important that everyone was screened before being allowed into the shelter program this year. They appreciated knowing that everybody in the shelter was assessed to be reasonably safe and able to maintain safe behavior.

**Phil:** Makes sense. I would hope that the "service" component might lead to greater ownership from the guests.

**Kacky:** Yes, the topic of "jobs" was mentioned. Many guests mentioned they wanted to have jobs and that everyone in the shelter should have a job.

**Phil:** Yes. I hope that happens next season. My last question is "What 'magic' happened for you this season, if any?"

**Kacky:** There was a lot of magic that happened such as witnessing the tenacity, strength, and growth in our guests as they faced almost insurmountable challenges, and working with volunteers over a long (164 nights) shelter season to provide compassion, humor, warmth, food and safety was magical.

I also think the level of your leadership was magical. I watched you work equally well with the guests, the volunteers, the city, OHRA, ACRC staff and the county. You appeared to work tirelessly with many of your weeks being 80+ hours long. It was interesting to watch. You were everywhere working with individual guests, community partners, volunteers, city and county staff, writing grants, opening the Extreme Weather Warming Center, negotiating lease details on the new One Site shelter building, and generally keeping everything operational.

I remember thinking "This man is going to crash and become very ill. He's working too much." There was so much to do, but you managed it. You pulled it all together so well. That was wonderful.

**Phil:** Your chicken noodle soup was part of my self-care program that appeared at the perfect moment when I was losing my voice and possibly coming down with something. Thanks for noticing!

**Kacky:** I learned a lot from watching you in process and how you showed compassion for all of the guests. You created a personal relationship with each guest and always gave them time to explain their side of a story without judgment. They felt connected to you because you reached out. They knew you cared! The same is true with the volunteers. I think that's a marvelous accomplishment.

You really put a lasso around the whole project and roped it in. And it was done. Now, the Ashland Winter Shelter is ready to move into the next iteration with newly hired staff members and a new forty-nine bed shelter building set up for the next three years. You really did it. That's pretty cool.

**Phil:** Very cool indeed. Thank you!

# Calls To Action

*"When one tugs at a single thing in nature, one finds it attached to the rest of the world."* ~John Muir

I hope you are inspired from the stories in this book to take some sort of action to end homelessness in your community. Perhaps it's your own personal version of "finding gloves for Matt."

Perhaps you could take an active role in customizing your community's solution by being involved in one or more of these 3 steps:

1. Humanize
2. Stabilize
3. Self-Actualize

Perhaps you will take notice of shifts in your community's thinking like that which happened here in Ashland:

- Mindset Shift 1 - From-Old-to-New-Model
- Mindset Shift 2 - From-Problem-to-Opportunity
- Mindset Shift 3 - From-Silos-to-Community-Partnerships

Perhaps there is a Listening Project in your future.

I imagine that there will be plenty of AHA and WOW moments for you and your community! Celebrate these!

I'd love to hear from you! Please connect with me at LinkedIn.com/in/PhilJohncock.

Best of Success,

Phil Johncock
Consultant
Ashland, Oregon

# Postscript: It Can Happen To Anyone

*"Although homelessness can happen to anyone, it just wasn't expected."* ~Linda Lewis, Vocalist

Tragedy struck my own family a month before my job as Shelter Consultant started. My mom (81) and dad (90) suddenly became homeless.

My father returned to his home in rural Michigan to find the stove on fire. Thinking he could put it out by himself, he went outside to grab the watering hose. When he returned, the fire had spread up the wall and had rapidly engulfed the roof of their modular home. Poof! Within minutes, their house burned down.

The good news is that everyone is safe. The bad news is that they had no fire insurance to rebuild. It was a total loss!

Mom and dad were now homeless. I never imagined this would happen to my beloved parents!

Likewise, every person who is homeless in your community has a unique and equally tragic story about how they became homeless in the first place. Homelessness can happen to anyone at any time!

It is "what happens next in response to homelessness" that really matters most.

In my case, the tragic loss of their home and homelessness served as a wake-up call, a "call to action" for the community (of loved ones around them) to step up and unite our efforts to take care of mom and dad, very quickly. Their sons (my brothers and I) set up weekly (or as often as needed) conference calls to discuss their most pressing needs and the specific action steps that were required for us to support our parents.

Unfortunately, most homeless people do not enjoy a family of children or relatives around them who step up to support them. Fortunately, if you're reading this, you're probably part of a community that is heeding the "call to action" to step up to take care of your unhoused neighbors.

In the Ashland community, good neighbors have been stepping up for the last 11 years during the freezing cold winter nights, when our new and chronic unhoused neighbors tell us the biggest challenge is "getting and staying warm."

In an article published by *Ashland Tidings* (August 26, 2018), I wrote, "For my parents, their most immediate post-fire needs were food, clothing and shelter (Maslow's hierarchy). My brother Mark took dad to a local food bank. Goodwill donated clothing. Red Cross provided money for a hotel for two nights; family covered costs of the next two weeks at a hotel nearby."

Fast-forward twelve months. As a result of our family community addressing immediate, short-term and long-term needs of my parents, mom now enjoys full Medicaid coverage and loves the nursing home where she has been staying for the last 10 months. I heard that she is even putting on weight, which is unusual with people with severe dementia.

To be able to visit daily his bride of 66 years, dad now lives with my youngest brother Mark who has an apartment in the same small town of a

102

little over 7,000 residents where the nursing home (taking care of my mom) is located (Hastings, Michigan).

I wonder what the situation will be like for your unhoused neighbors in the next 12 months as a result of you taking to heart the "call to action" and "stepping up" in your community!

# Appendixes

Appendix A - "One Site" Frequently Asked Questions (FAQs)
Appendix B - Letter from Kelly Shelter (September 2018)
Appendix C - Guest Agreement Form
Appendix D - Incident Report

# Appendix A - "One Site" Frequently Asked Questions (FAQs)

### What is the One Site committee?

The goal of the One Site Committee is to find one site for winter shelter in Ashland OR for 50 guests starting in November 2018. June 27, 2018 will be our 7th meeting (7 pm at the Ashland library). The committee meets every three weeks. Sub-committees meet weekly. One Site investigates "every" option so that no rock is left unturned and every alternative explored.

One Site is a temporary shelter opportunity for the next two winter seasons (Nov 2018 - Apr 2019 and Nov 2019 - Apr 2020) while a permanent shelter in Ashland is being planned, funded and built.

### What are the sub-committees of the One Site committee?

Alternatives, Budget/Fundraising, Car Parking, Emergency, Fast Track, Food/Meals, Government Planning, Governor Declaration, Intake/Data, Listening Project

### Who runs Ashland's Winter Shelter?

Unique as Ashland, shelters have been run by an inspiring collaboration of community partners including faith-based organizations like Unitarian Universalists (UU's), United Congregational Church of Christ (UCC), South Mountain Friends Meeting (Quakers), First Presbyterian Church, Temple Emek Shalom, Trinity Episcopal; the City of Ashland; nonprofits such as Southern Oregon Jobs With Justice, Options for Helping Residents of Ashland (OHRA) and Ashland Culture of Peace Commission (ACPC); and a cadre of committed, community volunteers. It takes a village to raise a shelter!

## What are the demographics of Ashland's homeless?

Highlights from the first ever Guest Intake Interviews conducted of 57 shelter guests over six nights in December 2017 and January 2018 illustrate the severity of the Ashland homeless crisis:

- 54% are disabled.
- The average length of time being homeless is 46.6 months.
- The average age is 44.2. The youngest is 23. The oldest is 72.
- 28% are considered "chronic homeless" (at least 4 years).
- 25% are female.
- 17.5% are veterans.

Many people believe that the homeless should be most interested in getting a job or finding housing. To guests, it's much more immediate like "what's for dinner?" In the freezing cold of winter nights, the biggest challenge they tell us is "getting and staying warm."

Unfortunately, Ashland has not collected accurate, real-time data on shelter guests in the past. Building on the results from these interviews, the Intake/Data sub-committee is working on a single point of entry with flexible entry alternatives and a mandatory pre-screening process for all guests.

Intake will be a new, formal intake procedure for every person using the shelter. This will allow us to know better who we are working with and help us to design individualized programs to help each person move on and get the services they need.

The intake process can be started during the summer of 2018. There is no need to wait until winter. The goal is to collect and maintain real-time data that can be used to coordinate care, manage our operations, better serve our guests and demonstrate successes and accountability to funders and the community.

**What is the required and preferred criteria for One Site?**

Required Criteria
- ❏ Capacity for 50 guests
- ❏ 2,200 square feet total with minimum of 34 square feet per guest
- ❏ Sprinklers that meet fire codes
- ❏ Minimum of 2 bathrooms
- ❏ Meets Americans with Disabilities Act (ADA) of 1990 standards
- ❏ Be available starting November 2018

Preferred Criteria
- ❏ Inexpensive insurance
- ❏ Place to serve food and clean up (sink, kitchen, refrigerator, etc.)
- ❏ Access to showers
- ❏ Access to laundry facilities
- ❏ Storage for linen, kitchen/toilet supplies and ideally guest backpacks/items
- ❏ Access to bus line
- ❏ Separate space for men and women/children

**What is the sense of urgency of finding One Site?**

There is an increased sense of urgency to find ONE site by the end of July 2018. The City of Ashland requires up to 3 months to approve applications for "conditional use permits," so the latest that pre-applications can be submitted is around August 1, 2018.

Cold weather and freezing nights will be here before we know it. If ONE site is not found, our downtown streets may be the only option for many of Ashland's homeless.

**Is there a long-term, permanent solution to address homelessness in Ashland?**

Absolutely. Options for Helping Residents of Ashland (OHRA) has purchased a property on Washington Street and is conducting a feasibility study of the site. The soonest a permanent shelter might be available is 2020. One Site is a temporary solution for 50 prioritized guests for the next two winter seasons (Nov 2018 - Apr 2019 and Nov 2019 - Apr 2020) while a permanent shelter is being planned, funded and built.

**What are the dates of One Site? How many nights per week? How many weeks? How many months?**

As a temporary solution while a permanent one is being planned, One Site is needed for 50 prioritized guests for the next two winter seasons: November 2018 - April 2019 and November 2019 - April 2020. One Site is offered ideally seven (7) nights per week for approximately 22 weeks starting in mid-November and ending mid-April. Hopefully, an extra week or two at the beginning and end of the season will allow for set up and clean up. One Site should be operational for 5 months.

**What are the hours of winter shelter at One Site?**

During the 2017-2018 shelter season, doors opened at 7:30 pm in the evening with lights out at 9:30 pm. Guests were up by 6-6:30 am the next morning and out-the-door by 7:30 am. Of course, these times may be adjusted as needed.

**What is the timeline for finding and setting up One Site?**

There is an increased sense of urgency to find one site by the end July 2018. The City of Ashland requires up to 3 months to approve applications for "conditional use permits," so the latest that pre-applications can be submitted is around August 1, 2018. Once the One Site has been secured, plans can move forward for setting up and staffing One Site. The mandatory "intake process" for guests is being planned by the Intake/Data sub-committee to be launched during the summer 2018 ahead of opening the shelter.

**As we depend on income from renting our facility, do you have funding to pay for rent?**

Absolutely. The Budget/Fundraising sub-committee has included rent, repair, and maintenance costs into the One Site budget. Other expenses may be added as well.

**How is "insurance" covered for One Site?**

The cost for insurance is included in the One Site budget. If One Site is a city-owned property, the City of Ashland may be able to cover some or all of the insurance costs.

**Where will funding come from to operate One Site?**

It's important to value the contribution of our volunteers first! Building on the record-setting 2017-2018 winter shelter season, over $100,000 in in-kind contributions (over 4,000 hours) will be provided by our committed volunteers.

In addition, since we're expanding from four (2017) to seven nights of shelter (2018), new strategies will be required to recruit greater numbers of trainees and co-hosts who are able and willing to spend the night. The Ashland Culture of Peace Commission (ACPC) has applied for a grant from the Carpenter Foundation (pending) to assist with recruitment and training of volunteers.

In addition, identified funding sources include a $25,000 grant from ACCESS (approved) and potential funding from a City block grant, housing trust fund, faith-based and business donations, community fundraisers, etc. The Budget/Fundraising sub-committee is organizing fundraising efforts.

**What would the responsibilities be in addition to providing the space?**

Additional responsibilities include 1) communicating concerns and questions, 2) willingness to liaison with the neighborhood and 3) participate, as necessary, with shelter leadership in identifying and addressing the most challenging and pressing issues (i.e., loitering, neighbor complaints, enforcing rules, etc.) quickly and responsibly.

The shelter leadership has a proven track record for addressing problems quickly and collectively. Eleven site coordinators brainstorm responsible, coordinated and sustainable solutions regularly. During the winter shelter season, shelter leadership meets monthly to coordinate operations, emails daily, and keeps its finger on the pulse of the guests, volunteers and site.

One Site will do all the heavy lifting by paying rent, covering any additional costs (i.e., insurance, repairs, toilet paper, kitchen utensils, etc.), staffing the shelter with volunteers and facilitating community-based problem-solving.

**What training and supervision is provided for shelter volunteers?**

Volunteer co-hosts who spend the night with guests must pass a background check every two years, which is conducted by the Ashland Police Department. Trainees apprentice with experienced hosts until they are comfortable to be a co-host. Orientations are provided to train volunteers, and a video of the orientation is provided to prospective volunteers. Volunteers also can serve in a variety of roles before and in addition to hosting such as listening, serving food, cleaning up, etc. Volunteers are supervised by co-hosts, site coordinators and the Coordinator of Volunteers.

**What are the most important "neighborhood" concerns related to One Site for 50 homeless guests? How do you plan to address these concerns?**

"Neighborhood" concerns are addressed one-by-one by the One Site committee, sub-committees, and shelter leadership on a regular basis. A few concerns expressed to date and solutions are:

1.  Behavioral Issues - According to the U.S. Department of Health & Human Services Substance Abuse and Mental Health Services Administration programs and services, "in January 2016, one in five people experiencing homelessness had a serious mental illness, and a similar percentage had a chronic substance use disorder. Discipline problems often occur as a result." A mandatory intake process will ensure that prospective guests are screened. Immediately, our unhoused can be referred to appropriate mental health, substance abuse, employment, housing and other services. All guests will be aware of shelter rules (see appendix), as well as consequences of breaking rules including losing one's bed at the shelter. Strict and prompt enforcement of shelter and city rules demonstrates zero tolerance for bad behavior.

2.  Loitering - Problems often occur when guests congregate on the property before or after shelter. To eliminate loitering, 1) day-time alternatives will attract guests away like "warming centers," "training centers," 12-step programs, employment opportunities and wellness services, 2) site rules may include an arrival time and a requirement to vacate the property by an agreed-upon time, and 3) security can be hired to help enforce site rules and ensure safety.

3.  No Barrier Entry - Ashland's shelter is a "housing first" model unlike shelters that require sobriety to enter. A mandatory intake process will ensure guests are pre-screened and appropriate substance-use services recommended prior to entry into a shelter. No alcohol or drugs will be tolerated on site. Guests who break rules will be immediately asked to leave and escorted out.

4. Supervision - The city provides free background checks of all co-hosts spending the night. At least two co-hosts (and often trainees) spend the night.

All efforts will be made to prevent problems and bad behavior. If issues arise, through a proven system of clear and ongoing communication between site coordinators and shelter leadership, each one is addressed promptly on a case-by-case basis.

**What do the homeless guests do during the day?**

Best practices of successful shelters elsewhere in our state and country point to the importance of guests checking out in the morning and participating in wellness activities during the day. Community leaders have expressed interest in day "warming centers," "training centers" and activities designed to support guest goals of employment, housing, life skills, wellness, etc. The Ashland Community Resource Center will provide case management to assist guests during the day with mental health referrals, Ashland Job Match services, housing alternatives, etc.

**What are the Shelter Guidelines or rules?**

- Check-in begins at approximately 7:30 pm.
- No drugs, alcohol or weapons.
- No threatening or abusive language.
- No disruptive behavior.
- No excessive noise, including loud radios and loud phone conversations.
- Guests must arrive before 9:30 pm, when doors will be locked, lights turned off.
- No smoking inside. Smoking outside is restricted to designated areas.
- No smoking breaks after doors are locked.
- Anyone leaving the building after 9:30 pm will not be readmitted.
- No guests allowed in the kitchen.
- No storage of personal belongings.

- Guests must vacate the building and property by 7:30 am except when assisting with clean up and supervised by a site volunteer.

Failure to comply with Shelter Guidelines or rules may result in a temporary or permanent ban of a guest from future stays and a forfeiture of a guest's bed.

# Appendix B - Letter from Kelly Shelter

September 14, 2018

Attn: Phil Johncock

Dear Phil,

As the Kelly Shelter Case Manager in 2018, I witnessed a decrease in crime and an increase in both personal responsibility and respectful attitudes for area the shelter was occupied. Kelly Shelter rules were kept simple, "Be respectful to yourself and others", to keep it very basic. We had very little problems with guests.

The homeless community were very grateful for the opportunity to be housed and having immediate access to resources. There were several businesses directly across the street that were not aware that the shelter was even open for a couple weeks, and then it wasn't because of problems, but of structured times services were offered.

The guests took pride in the privilege to be housed. They would pick up around the areas we occupied and cleaned up after themselves fairly well. The baggage (carts, tents, bedrolls, sleeping bags) that in most cases homeless bring with them were not present this year, as we provided a storage container for them to be placed in.

Respectfully,


Brandie Barnes
Kelly Shelter Case Manager

# Appendix C - Guest Agreement Form

*(Many thanks to Chad McComas, Executive Director with Rogue Retreat, and Brandie Barnes, Case Manager, with the Kelly Shelter, for their permission to revise the Kelly Shelter Guest Agreement Form for use at Ashland's Winter Shelter.)*

By signing this form, I agree to the following:
I will have respect for neighbors and everyone at or associated with the overnight shelter at all times, including staff, Night Coordinators, hosts, listeners, food servers, clean up crew, any volunteer, other guests, and the general public. This means that I will not be disrespectful, violent, disruptive, vulgar or combative in any way. Bullying will not be tolerated.

I will have respect for the surrounding neighborhoods of all shelter sites as I come and go to and from the shelter, including picking up my garbage and cigarette butts along the way. Shopping carts and bike trailers will not be allowed inside the shelter or outside on the property. I understand that all carts on the property will be disposed of with no warning. Bikes must be stored at the bike rack, if one is available.

I understand that shelter and community partners are not responsible for loss or stolen items, so I agree to secure them at my own risk.

I agree to inform co-hosts (only) at least one night before I know I will be absent. I understand that two unexcused absences means that I will lose my bed at the shelter and must get back in line to be considered for a bed if and when an opening comes available.

I understand the shelter doors will be locked between the hours of 9:30 pm and 6:00 am. I may choose to leave during these hours (smoke break, etc.) but I will not be allowed back in until doors reopen the next morning. I agree not to sleep outside on the property or in the neighborhood. I agree to leave the shelter properties by 7:00 am.

I acknowledge that if my minor child(ren) are admitted to the shelter with me, they are solely my responsibility. The shelter staff and volunteers are not responsible to supervise, provide parental discretion or care for them.

I will not bring any alcohol or drugs or drug paraphernalia inside the shelter or onto properties.

I will not smoke inside the building or on the properties (including e-cigarettes) except in designated smoking areas at least 20 feet away from the building.

I will not carry any banned weapons (i.e., guns, knives, explosive devices, etc.) onto the properties. I understand that shelter staff are fully authorized to make determinations regarding such items on a case-by-case basis.

I will not be allowed to bring guests onto the properties. I will not engage in any sexual activity with myself or anyone else inside the shelter or on the properties.

If there is a problem or concern, I will find a co-host or Night Coordinator on duty to handle it.

I understand that if I have a physical emergency, staff may call 911 to help me.

I understand that if I am asked to leave the shelter for my behavior, I must have permission from staff to come on the properties.

These agreements make Ashland's Winter Shelter safe for everyone and ensure that it can continue to be open. I understand that breaking any of these agreements will be dealt with immediately and may result in my removal from the shelter, and I may be placed on a permanent ban.

_____

Print Name

_____

Sign Name

_____

Date

# Appendix D - Incident Report Form

(*Many thanks to Leigh Madsen, Executive Director with the Ashland Community Resource Center, for his input in the development of this form.*)

Violation of Ashland's Winter Shelter rules & safety policies:

| | | |
|---|---|---|
| ❏ Bullying | ❏ Dogs/Animals | ❏ Smoking |
| ❏ Combative | ❏ Drug/Alcohol Use | ❏ Violent |
| ❏ Disrespectful | ❏ Loitering | ❏ Vulgar |
| ❏ Disruptive | ❏ Noise | ❏ Other: Specify |

_____

Person Submitting Report_____

Name of Offender_____

Date_____ Time_____ Location_____

Briefly Describe What Happened (continue on back if necessary)

_____

_____

_____

_____

Resulting Action Taken:     __Warning by whom?_____ ...when?_____

__Other: Specify_____

Date Returned to Consultant_____

# About the Author

Phil Johncock has helped 1,000's of U.S. nonprofits over the last 40 years to become fully sustainable. For example, in just 5 ½ months, he secured over $1 million in funding that can be used for three years for Ashland's Winter Shelter for the homeless.

Phil has written 26 books (this is the 26th). A genius completer, Phil authored and published 11 books in 3 years (2003-3006) and 11 more books in 3 months in 2017 (January - March). He co-authored with best-selling authors Dr. Gay Hendricks and Jack Canfield (*Book of Life* and *Already Home*) and Margot Anand (*Sexual Ecstasy Workbook: Path of SkyDancing Tantra*) and posthumously collaborating with his Great Grandma Zelpha to publish the diary she wrote between 1935 and 1940 (*Zelpha's Secret Diary*).

Phil is a genius in designing sustainable, model programs. For example, he created a 10-credit college grant writing certification program that resulted in $1.2 billion in grant funding in just 2.5 years for hundreds of local students and nonprofits. It is still operating today.

Many have relied on him to "take their organizations to the next level." For example, in 2010-2015, Phil was approached by Charles Schwab Bank to become the Executive Director for the Alliance for Nevada Nonprofits creating a virtual business model, saving the Nevada nonprofit sector almost $2 million and providing 21,105 hours of professional development to 6,762 nonprofit leaders.

An innovator in online education, Phil designed the first grant writing class on the Internet in 1997 (GrantWritingBasics.com) and the 30-Day Fast Track (GrantWritingFastTrack.com).

For fun, Phil enjoys ecstatic dancing and making up impromptu celebratory songs on-the-spot while playing his acoustic guitar.

Phil Johncock

Connect with Phil at LinkedIn.com/in/PhilJohncock.

www.ingramcontent.com/pod-product-compliance
Lightning Source LLC
Chambersburg PA
CBHW072053280526
45788CB00006B/2276